THE QUILTER'S GUIDE TO
AMISH
QUILTS

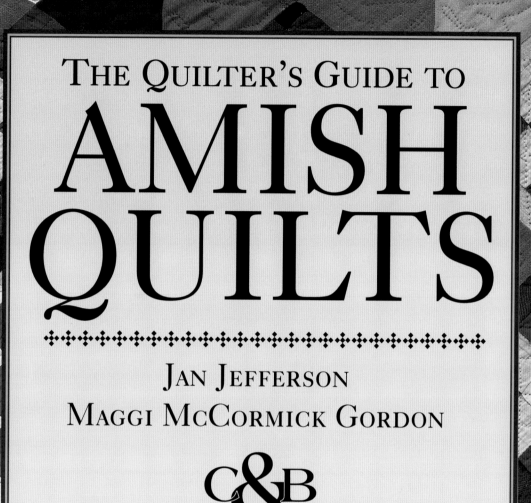

THE QUILTER'S GUIDE TO
AMISH QUILTS

•◆•◆•◆•◆•◆•◆•◆•◆•◆•◆•◆•◆•◆•◆•◆•◆•◆•

JAN JEFFERSON
MAGGI McCORMICK GORDON

C&B
COLLINS & BROWN

First published in Great Britain in 1998
by Collins & Brown Limited
London House
Great Eastern Wharf
Parkgate Road
London SW11 4NQ

1 3 5 7 9 8 6 4 2

British Library Cataloguing-in-Publication Data:
A catalogue record for this book is available from the British Library.

ISBN 1 85585 612 3 (hardback edition)

ISBN 1 85585 655 7 (paperback edition)

Conceived, edited and designed by Collins & Brown Limited
Editorial Director: Sarah Hoggett
Art Director: Roger Bristow
Editors: Katie Bent and Lisa Dyer
Senior Art Editor: Julia Ward-Hastelow
Photography: Matthew Ward
Illustrator: Kate Simunek

Reproduction by Hong Kong Graphics
Printed and bound in Hong Kong

Half-title page: Diamond in the Square, Lancaster County, 1920-30 (Quilt, Private Collection;
photograph courtesy The Quilt Complex, Oakland, CA)
Title page: Nine-Patch variation (detail), Mifflin County, 1920-30 (Quilt, Private Collection;
photograph courtesy The Quilt Complex, Oakland, CA)

Jacket illustrations:
Front cover: Sunshine and Shadow Quilt, Ohio, *c.* 1930 (Quilt, Private Collection;
photograph courtesy The Quilt Complex, Oakland, CA)
Back cover (top center): © Jerry Irwin

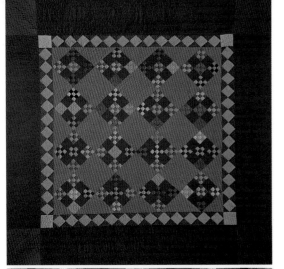

Contents

Introduction

✦✦✦✦✦✦✦✦✦✦✦✦✦✦✦✦✦✦✦

*D*RIVING ON THE BACK roads of Lancaster County, Pennsylvania, is an unusual experience. Much of the time your car might be the only one on the road, but there is another conveyance: the horse and buggy. When you look into the farmers' fields that surround you, horses and mules are pulling the plow, the seed drill, and the harvesting equipment. There is little evidence of modern life. This is Amish country, quiet, peaceful and slow; a place that has given rise to some of the most intriguing and artistic quilts in the United States.

THE HISTORY OF THE AMISH PEOPLE

In their beauty and simplicity, Amish quilts offer a unique insight into the history and traditions of the "Plain" people. The story of the Amish starts nearly 500 years ago, at the time of the Protestant Reformation in Europe. In 1525, a group of Swiss Reformers, known as Anabaptists, introduced the doctrine that baptism could be received only by adults

Center Diamond, *c.* 1920
This outstanding example of a traditional Amish pattern demonstrates spectacular use of color with uninhibited combinations typical of Lancaster County.

who chose to join the fellowship. In 1536 a Dutch Anabaptist leader, Menno Simons, founded a nonviolent group, known as Mennonites. By the late seventeenth century, the followers of a Swiss Mennonite Elder, Jacob Ammann, considered the Mennonites to be moving away from their original principles. The difference over doctrine caused a division in 1693 and of a new group was formed, called the Amish, after Ammann.

At the end of the seventeenth century, Amish and Mennonite groups, suffering from persecution and famine, were contacted by William Penn, a Quaker who had received a land grant in the New World. He decided to use Pennsylvania for a "great experiment": to see if people of different religions could live together harmoniously. The first Amish groups arrived from Germany in the 1720s, with nearly 100 families traveling to Pennsylvania by the 1750s. By the nineteenth century, the Amish had moved out to other states such as Indiana, Ohio, Iowa, and Kansas.

This history is still evident in the lives of modern-day Amish communities. The Lancaster County Amish still speak a dialect of Swiss German among themselves, and because of the language difference, historically they have referred to outsiders – their non-Amish neighbors, tourists, and foreign visitors – as "English." Their strong religious beliefs guide them through every choice in their daily lives, following the doctrine of the Bible. A strong sense of family and community is taught from an early age, based on the values of shared brotherhood, honesty, and love. Their plain lifestyle, based on practicality and humility, still guides them through the modern world.

Through their language, dress, and lifestyle the Amish strive to keep themselves separate from the outside world – if not literally, then certainly spiritually.

The Horse and Buggy
This is a familiar sight in Lancaster County, Pennsylvania. The use of horse power to pull the buggy, and the windmill against the skyline, reflect the Amish rejection of modern or "worldly" machinery.

THE AMISH QUILTING TRADITION

Early Amish quilts were purely functional. They were not made to be beautiful or decorative. The winters were long and cold, and patchwork quilts were a practical, frugal way to keep warm. All clothing was homemade, and hence the scrap basket was the first source of fabric for a new quilt. The Amish, like all the early American settlers, were careful to avoid wasting any commodity. Patchworking was the sort of frugal craft that fitted perfectly into the lives of these farming people.

Amish quilts were made in the plain, dark colors of Amish clothing, primarily blue, green, purple, burgundy, brown, gray, and black. These dark colors were inexpensive to buy and needed infrequent washing, a practical advantage for the quiltmaker. Lancaster County Amish quilts were somber in cool shades with wide use of dark blue, while Midwestern Amish women used warmer colors combined with black.

Traditional Amish patchwork was basic; the simple geometric shapes of squares, rectangles, and triangles were used. These shapes were easy and quick to fit together. Many of the geometric patterns used in Amish quilts are logical developments of trial and error with form and color. Early patchwork patterns ranged from the large fields of the Center Diamond to smaller pieced quilts, such as Tumbling Blocks and Sunshine and Shadow.

The early style of quilting was designed simply to hold the quilt together and prevent the batting (wadding) from slipping between the front and back pieces. Quilting was carried out in straight lines or in crosshatching, to hold the

Scrap quilt, 1980
This is the ultimate Amish scrap quilt, making use of many different fabrics. Even in the late twentieth century, Amish quilters are still being led by practicality and frugality.

batting securely in place. As time went on, quiltmaking became an important exercise for the Amish. Like all the tasks they turned their hand to, it was accomplished with great skill and expertise. Amish quilts became more and more sophisticated, and the later quilts are distinguished by their bold compositions in intense colors and large fields of fabric embellished with ornate quilting motifs.

By the late nineteenth century, most Amish homes had at least one good quilt, made from fine wool and quilted with small, intricate stitches. The beautiful quilts and fine stitching of today have their foundations in the late-nineteenth-century "best" quilts.

CHANGES IN TRADITION

Traditionally, quilts were made of wool or cotton. In recent years, however, the Amish have taken enthusiastically to using modern artificial fabrics. Because their own clothes are now made from both natural and artificial fabrics, their quilts may contain many different materials. Easy-care fabrics have become a preferred choice because they wash easily and do not need ironing. The fabric available in the scrap bag still defines the quilt.

Early batting consisted of pieces of wool stretched across the back of the patchwork top.

In the middle of the nineteenth century, cotton replaced wool and continued to be used until the mid-twentieth century when synthetic batting became popular. Fashions change, however, and some of the inventions of the twentieth century are now rejected by modern quiltmakers. Synthetic batting, which was hailed as a great innovation a few years ago, is now being replaced by cotton.

By the middle of the twentieth century a few changes had taken place in Amish patchwork. The use of block patchwork and patchwork designs that depicted objects such as baskets, stars, and houses were two of these changes. Importantly, however, the Amish still used scrap fabric and limited themselves to a narrow range of colors.

In the early 1960s outside influences began to alter life for the Amish quiltmaker. Tourism came to many Amish communities, and visitors from all over the United States began to discover Amish quilts in ever-increasing numbers. Although people were impressed with the patterns and workmanship, the colors were not always to modern taste, and Amish women were asked to make quilts in fancy fabrics supplied by the tourists. Because the Amish are not afraid of commerce and realized that quilts could provide income, more and more Amish

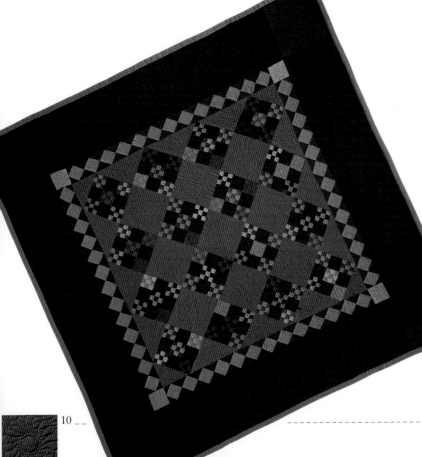

Double Nine-Patch, c. 1930
The range of colors used in this quilt echoes the scrap quilts of the 1800s. The beauty of the piece comes from the random placing of color and the superb quilting. The double nine-patch blocks have been placed on point to create a diamond effect, a popular shape with Amish quilters.

women began making quilts to order. Finally some decided that buying fabric in pretty prints and making quilts speculatively might be a good idea. Signs advertising "Quilts for Sale" began appearing outside Amish farms.

New ideas continue to interest the Amish quilter; their most recent change has been to adopt appliqué techniques, such as the Lancaster Rose pattern (see page 103). This decorative process is popular with both makers and buyers, and large numbers are produced for sale. For the most part, however, in their homes the Amish continue to use the plain quilts of their tradition.

HOW TO USE THIS BOOK

The quilts featured in this book are typical of Amish design and each one exemplifies in some way an aspect of Amish life and culture. The ten chapters feature a particular pattern that illustrates the changing style of Amish quilting and patchwork. Antique and modern examples are given, showing the beautiful range of colors and exquisite quilting that typifies Amish work. These examples can be used as an inspiration for color combinations and suggestions for motifs for your own quilts.

The projects at the end of each chapter are shown in photographs, in step-by-step sequence. All the information that you need to complete the quilt is either shown in the steps or cross-referenced to the basic techniques section at the back of the book (pages 112–17). The projects are suitable for quilters of all abilities, although the beginner may wish to start with the simpler quilts, such as the Bars or Center Diamond, before tackling more complicated patterns.

Tumbling Blocks, 1980
This is a functional Amish baby quilt made in practical colors from a traditional pattern that relies on small pieces. Geometric patterns are popular with Amish quilters because they make use of small scraps of fabric. The unusual use of green and terracotta borders was occasioned by the fabrics in the scrap basket at the time.

Patchwork templates and quilting motifs for the projects are also included on pages 118–25. Use the diagram included in the project as a guide to positioning the motifs. You can, of course use different motifs from those suggested in the book.

When making the quilts, follow the cutting guides carefully. A chart giving the total amount of fabric required, and the finished size of the quilt, is included on page 126. Always use either standard (imperial) or metric measurements, never a mix of the two.

Bars

❖ ❖ ❖ ❖ ❖ ❖ ❖ ❖ ❖

THE BARS QUILT IS ONE of the most traditional of Amish patterns. Consisting of strips, or bars, of fabric in two or more alternating colors, the Bars quilt represents one of the fundamental values of the Amish: simplicity. Early quiltmakers were discouraged by the church from creative, artistic patchwork, so most of the patterns were simplistic in terms of design and color, and the Bars, along with the Center Diamond, Sunshine and Shadow, and Nine-Patch, is a good example of this. The colors used for the pattern range from shades of blue, red or burgundy, purple, gray, brown, and green. The borders surrounding the bars are usually dark blue; black is used infrequently.

The design was one of the easiest for the early Amish settlers to complete. Because the winters were long and bitterly cold, and each bed had three or four quilts, a large number of quilts was needed in every home. Rather than laboriously cutting strips up into smaller blocks or other shapes, lengths of cotton fabric were joined together to make the quilt. This quick and economical method of working was probably just a shortcut to making yet another quilt for a bed. Because the Bars quilt is visually and

Bars, c. 1920
The moss-green borders in this quilt are unusual for the Lancaster County Amish, but their width and the corner blocks lie perfectly in the Lancaster tradition.

structurally the simplest of the Amish quilts, it adapts perfectly to all sorts of uses in an Amish home: a full-size quilt was used on a bed; a smaller size as a lap quilt or crib quilt; and a small square functioned as a potholder.

STRIP QUILTS

Amish women were inspired in their original patchwork by their non-Amish neighbors. Many of their fellow settlers came from the north of England and Wales, and these women were

making superb quilts with simple patchwork techniques; the echoes of their patterns can be seen in early Amish quilts. The Bars design closely resembles the Durham strip quilt, and the Center Diamond (see page 25), has its basis in traditional Welsh quilts.

The British strip, or "strippy" quilt, dating from the mid-1800s until about 1930, differed from the Bars quilt in that it had no border. The strips usually ran vertically and were odd in number so a main strip was central to the

This exquisitely stitched basket motif is one that is often found on Bars quilts.

Split Bars Quilt, *c.* 1910
The maker of this quilt has used soft pastel shades that harmonize well, and the color scheme in itself would be enough to recommend it. Unusually for a Bars quilt, the cross-hatching on the bars stops short of the center, creating a medallion effect that echoes motifs more often found on Center Diamond quilts. It is the quality of the quilting – the imaginative combination of motifs and the flowing lines used on both the inner and outer borders – that gives this particular quilt its appeal.

The vine, with its grapes, flows elegantly around the entire inner border.

The eight-point star in the middle is surrounded by three concentric rings of feathered cable and finished by a bold octagonal outline.

design. Like the Bars, strip quilts were embellished with long flowing quilting effects running the length of the strip, and were also usually made for purely utilitarian purposes by ordinary housewives.

QUILTING EFFECTS

The limited use of piecework on the Bars quilt allows vast areas of fabric on which to indulge elaborate quilting effects. The traditional quilting is crosshatching, which was done on all early quilts to hold the batting (wadding) and layers of fabric in place. The quilting needed to be extremely fine and close together, and crosshatching was the best stitching pattern for this purpose. The border, corner blocks, and inner border on the Bars design were also usually highlighted with intricate, carefully executed, quilting – a hallmark of Lancaster County Amish quilts.

Feathers, cables, vines, and leaves often appear in bars and borders because they adapt

Blocks and Bars, *c.* 1910
This antique quilt from Mifflin County, Pennsylvania, is a simple scrap quilt. The patchwork is made up in large blocks alternating with narrower bars. A wonderful variety of colors and shades are used, including somber browns and vibrant reds. The frugal use of scraps can be detected in the pieced borders. The quilting is also typical of a utilitarian quilt, with basic crosshatching over the entire pieced area and simple fan shapes on the borders.

Unusually, the corners are quilted differently from the borders using a diagonal "X" pattern.

The pieced bars are made of squares and sashing to give a thick-and-thin stack.

well to the linear structure, but many other motifs were also employed. The fernlike fiddlehead design is almost exclusively Amish, but stylized tulips and roses, possibly influenced by the Pennsylvania Dutch, also feature. However, animal designs are quite rare.

CORNER BLOCKS, SPLIT BARS, AND OTHER VARIATIONS

Although traditionally restricted in their choices of design, the Amish quiltmakers regularly varied basic patterns. Always frugal, they would use up the tiniest of scraps, which resulted in the introduction of more elaborate piecing. Other pieced or patchwork patterns often combined with the Bars to make more complicated quilts, such as rows of Flying Geese alternating with bars in solid colors. Nine-Patch or Four-Patch blocks are sometimes stacked to create the bars in the design, or alternate bars are made up from many coloured squares stacked vertically.

Split Bars, *c.* 1925–30
An unusual muted shade of gray-blue provides the key to this quilt and helps to tone down what might otherwise be a rather overpowering combination of red and pink. In contrast to the audacity of the colors, the quilting is traditional – crosshatching on the bars and swirling feathers on the borders.

The grapevine with grapes quilted on the inner border is emphasized by the larger bunches of fruit that appear on the corner squares.

It is unusual to see the pieced strips of the bars copied in the inner border.

Cool blue offsets the fiery red and pink.

A wide border, with corner blocks, is normally found on the traditional Bars quilt. A plain inner border also sometimes appears, acting as a frame for the bars. However, some rare versions use piecework in the inner border, an effect that serves to set off and emphasize the central bar design. The inner border may also consist of a split-bar pattern, or even contain corner blocks.

Although the Bars quilt is usually seen with corner blocks, there is also a version called Floating Bars, which does not have corner patches in the outer border – the result being that the central strips of bars appear to "float" on a plain field. The bars in the Split Bars design are divided by narrower bands of fabric in a contrasting color, which set off the main bars. All these variations allow a greater degree of experimentation with color, and fitting smaller blocks into the large strips in the Bars quilt conforms perfectly with Amish frugality and creativity.

Flying Geese Bars Quilt, 1990

Only a relatively small part of this quilt uses red fabric, but it is used so strikingly that the color leaps out. The stark contrast of dark blue and primary red is offset by the lighter blue of the bars and inner border. A hint of red in the binding pulls the whole quilt together and lightens what would otherwise be a very dark band of deep blue around the outer edge.

A thin strip of red binding is used to echo the red of the four center bars.

The flowing lines of the quilted cable design soften the precise, geometric shapes of the bars and flying geese triangles.

The triangular geese are simply outline-quilted.

Amish Family Life

*D*UE TO AN EARLY *history of persecution, the Amish take refuge in a close-knit community and strong family. The family is the core of Amish life and the most important part of their faith, supporting its members and keeping them strong in their separation from the outside world.*

Children are considered God's greatest gift, and marriage and procreation the ultimate aim of Amish people. All family members are important – disabled children are sheltered within the family; grandparents are honored and cared for. Parents instruct and set good moral examples for their children, and elder children are expected to set the same example to those younger. Respecting and obeying authority and helping others are important lessons. The children are raised to view their separateness from the world with pride.

Once children become teenagers, there is often a degree of rebellion, which is expected and accepted by the community. Teenagers experiment with worldly clothing, cinema, music, and even cars. This is referred to as "running around," and, though frowned upon, it is not a sin in the eyes of the church since the children have not yet been baptized. The Amish believe in freedom of choice and their members do not join the church until they

The family is the core of Amish life and the most important part of their faith.

make their own decision to do so, usually between the ages of seventeen and twenty-five. After their experience of "running around," over three-quarters of teenagers return to the faith. A period of prayer and instruction follows, then baptism. The children have been taught the Amish ways all their lives, and the Amish believe this strong foundation will guide them through their teenage years.

The Amish house is the focal point for the family. Many families have lived in the same house for generations, so they have strong ancestral ties. The Amish do not move for social reasons, nor do they aim for bigger homes in better locations. Although each nuclear family has its own house, the extended family is highly valued and lives as close as they can – either on the same farm or in the nearest small town. New houses are built as the family grows; for example, when a child marries or when the grandparents are ready to retire. A number of these individual houses may be

The Amish home is simply decorated.

joined together or positioned separately on the farm. If newly-marrieds choose not to live on the farm, then a house is built for them close by. The houses are finished with timber boarding or shingling, and then painted.

Hand-made furniture, such as serviceable chairs, tables, and dressers, equips the house. In every family there is a carpenter who makes the furniture; even the kitchen units if the house is new. There are no carpets on the floors, no curtains at the windows, no sofas or easy chairs. Nothing is fancy or decorative. The floors are scrubbed floorboards or linoleum with a few rag rugs for warmth. The windows are covered with simple dark green window shades (blinds). Walls are painted white, pale blue, or green, and hung with a calendar, a painted or embroidered family tree, and usually a lovely old clock – a traditional wedding gift.

The house is lit by compressed gas lamps hung from a hook in the ceiling, although oil lamps may also be used. Heating is provided by a wood-burning stove, fireplace, or butane (paraffin) heater. There are few modern appliances, and none of the entertainment, such as television, radio, or video, that the outside world takes for granted.

Though simple and utilitarian, Amish homes are also homely and comfortable. A big sitting-room, just off or possibly part of the kitchen, is the nucleus of the house. The room is furnished with a large table and chairs, a

Amish families spend as much time together as possible.

desk, and other small items. Here the family works, plays, and prays together, and here the visitor is entertained. The meals, and often the quiltmaking and sewing, take place here as well. Although there are other rooms in the house – a "gut" (good) room, a wash room, a pantry, and bedrooms, – the family uses one room predominantly: spending time together is the key to staying together.

Though simple and utilitarian, Amish homes are comfortable.

The Amish have a very strong work ethic, and the little free time they have is spent visiting family and friends, reading, or talking. Guests are always welcome and entertained by chatting, storytelling, and playing games while children sing songs and recite poetry. Food, such as freshly baked pies and cakes, pretzels, and candies, are always available. Evenings in the Amish home are spent very much as they would have been 100 years ago.

Making the Quilt

ECAUSE OF ITS inherent simplicity and straightforward design, the Bars quilt is a good project for the inexperienced quilter. The cutting can be done quickly with a rotary cutter, and the piecing is simply a matter of stitching a few straight seams. But it is the quilting that truly makes this quilt, so work with care to create an heirloom for the future.

Making the Quilt

CUTTING GUIDE

Piece	Quantity	Measurement
Corner squares	4 red	$8^{1}/2$ in (21cm)
Border strips	4 blue	$8^{1}/2 \times 26$ in (21 × 66 cm)
Center strips	3 purple 2 red 2 green	$4^{1}/4 \times 26^{1}/2$ in (11 × 67cm)
Backing	1 blue	44 in (112 cm) square – join widths if necessary

See page 126 for the total amount of fabric required to complete this quilt.

CUTTING

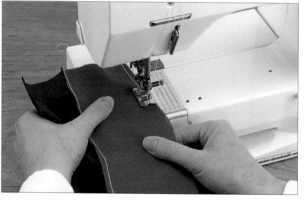

1 Following the instructions given in the Cutting Guide *(left)*, cut out the border and center strips and the corner squares *(see inset)*. As it is comprised of large, straight pieces, the Bars quilt is perfect for rotary cutting – though you can use scissors if you prefer.

STITCHING

2 First make the central bars section. Place the first two strips – a purple, then a red – right sides together and stitch, taking a $^{1}/4$-inch (6-mm) seam.

3 Place the third (green) strip right sides together with the second strip and stitch, starting at the end at which you finished the previous seam.

4 Stitch the remaining strips, referring to the photograph *(opposite)* for the correct order of colors. Press seams to one side.

5 Trim the pieced center section to level off the top and bottom, to create a true square *(see inset)*. Remember to place the ruler over the "good" part of the area being cut.

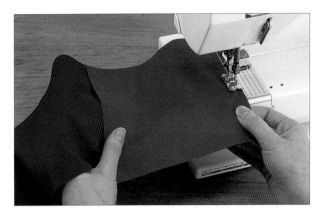

6 To make the border, place one red square at the end of one border strip, right sides together, and stitch taking a ¼-inch (6-mm) seam). Repeat to make four units.

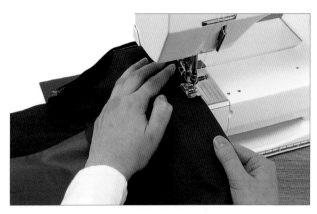

7 Place one border unit along the top edge of the center section, right sides together. The corner square should overhang the edge of the center section. Begin stitching about 2–3 inches (5–7.5 cm) from the corner of the center section.

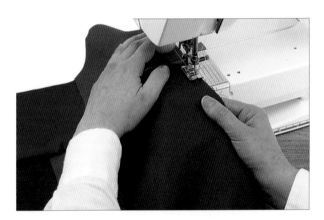

8 Place the second and subsequent border units along adjacent sides and stitch in place. Make sure that where corner squares meet the center section the seams are matched precisely.

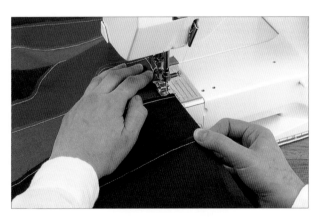

9 After the fourth border unit has been stitched in place, return to the overhanging corner square on the first border unit and finish stitching the seam.

10 Press all the seams to one side, working on the wrong side of the quilt. The finished quilt top is now ready to be marked with the quilting patterns.

MARKING

11 Mark the crosshatching in the center section first. Starting in one corner, use a ruler to draw diagonal straight lines from edge to edge. The lines on the rotary ruler can be used to line up subsequent lines.

12 Using the templates on page 122, mark all the quilting motifs. *Inset*: Mark as lightly as possible, but bear in mind that the marks must last until the quilting is finished.

13 The diagram above shows the position of the baskets and feathered circles on the border.

14 Add batting (wadding) and backing and baste (tack) the layers together *(see page 117)*. Work the quilting by hand, then remove the basting and bind the edges *(see page 117)*.

MEASUREMENT GUIDE
MAKING A 7-BAR QUILT IN A DIFFERENT SIZE

	Corner squares	Top/bottom borders	Center strips	Side borders
Cot (crib)	$4^{3}/8$ in (11 cm)	$19^{1}/4 \times 4^{3}/8$ in (49 × 11 cm)	$2^{3}/4 \times 33^{1}/4$ in (7 × 84.5 cm)	$4^{3}/8 \times 33^{1}/4$ in (11 × 84.5 cm)
Single (twin)	$11^{1}/2$ in (29 cm)	$11^{1}/2 \times 42$ in (29 × 107 cm)	$6 \times 78^{1}/2$ in (15 × 200 cm)	$11^{1}/2 \times 78^{1}/2$ in (29 × 200 cm)
Double (full)	12 in (30.5 cm)	12×56 in (30.5 × 142 cm)	8×66 in (20 × 168 cm)	12×66 in (30.5 × 168 cm)
Queen	$13^{1}/2$ in (34 cm)	$13^{1}/2 \times 63$ in (34 × 160 cm)	9×73 in (23 × 185 cm)	$13^{1}/2 \times 73$ in (34 × 185 cm)
King	20 in (51 cm)	20×70 in (51 × 178 cm)	10×70 in (25.5 × 178 cm)	20×70 in (51 × 178 cm)

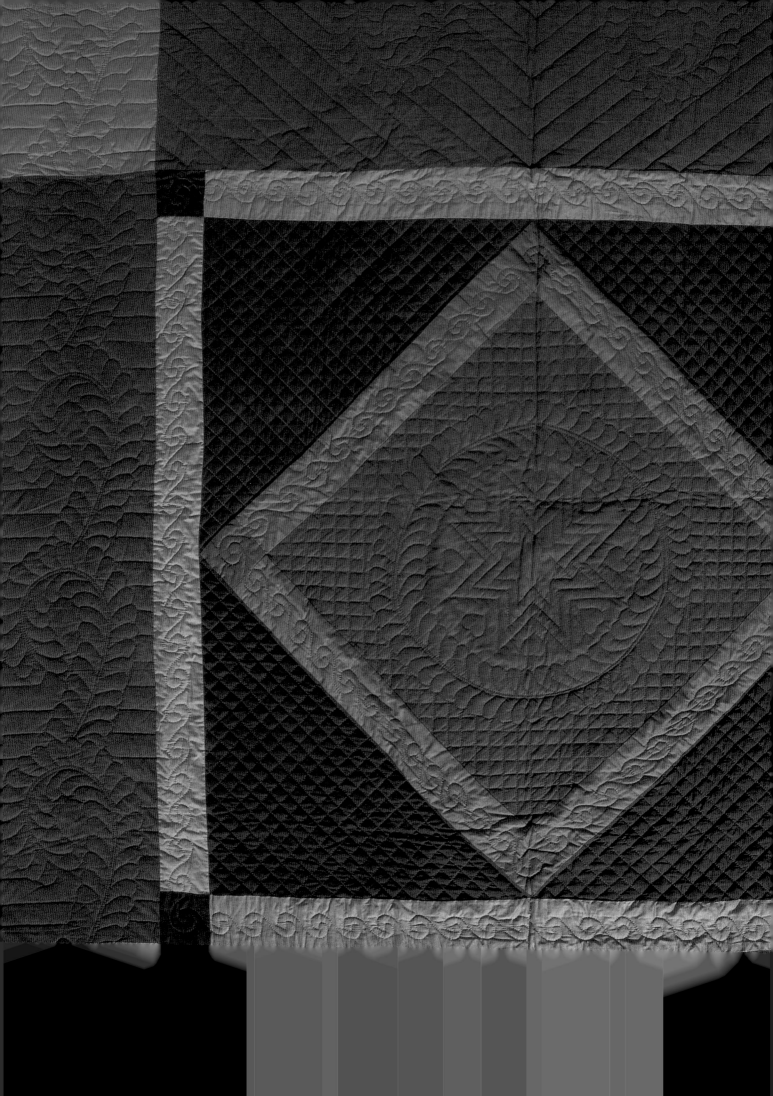

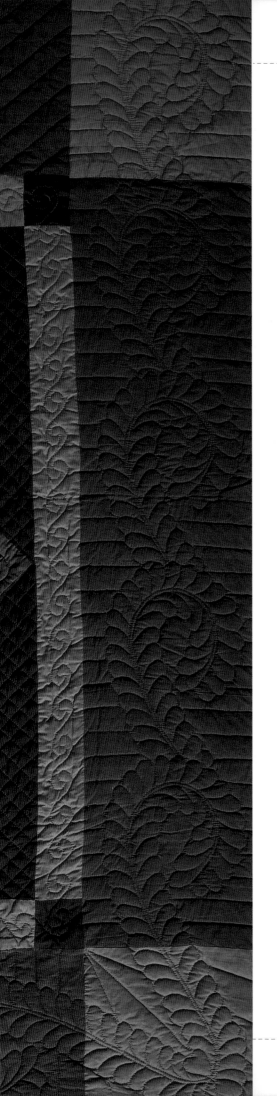

Center Diamond

❖❖❖❖❖❖❖❖❖❖❖❖❖❖❖❖❖❖❖❖❖❖❖❖❖

ALSO CALLED THE DIAMOND in the Square, this pattern exhibits all the hallmarks of Amish quilting, combining simply pieced patchwork in glowing colors with intricate hand quilting. Because Amish quilting started in eastern Pennsylvania, the early, more traditional, patterns, such as the Center Diamond, are most often found among the conservative Amish communities of Lancaster County. As it is so strongly identified with this area, any appearance elsewhere usually suggests a family connection.

In the nineteenth century, when more worldly quilt makers were vying with each other to produce quilts with the most and smallest patches, this pattern was an example of the importance that the Amish put on non-showmanship and humility. With its large blocks and triangles, the design is simple and clear. The bold pattern, strong colors, and such features as the large borders and corner blocks, are typical of Lancaster County quilts, and usually colors from the cool end of

Center Diamond, *c.* 1990
Five unpredictable colors are used in this magnificent quilt, giving vibrancy to a very traditional pattern, which is enhanced by the beautifully executed central star.

the spectrum are used, such as blues, purples, and greens. The pattern positions light fabrics against dark to make a compellingly graphic geometric configuration.

SOURCES OF FABRIC

Fabric for the Center Diamond quilt was traditionally woolen. It was probably bought or made specifically for the quilt, as the sizes of the pieces required for the large diamond are too large for scraps. Another source of readily available fabric may have been the Amish

women's capes – a triangular garment worn over the dress, covering the shoulders at the widest point of the triangle and coming to a point at the waist, front and back. These garments may have been taken apart and used for the large triangles, or pieced together to make up the central diamond patch.

By the twentieth century, cotton fabric was being introduced into all Amish quilts for the patchwork and backing, and cotton batting (wadding) for the filling. But the availability of fabric, not color or quality, still defined the quilt.

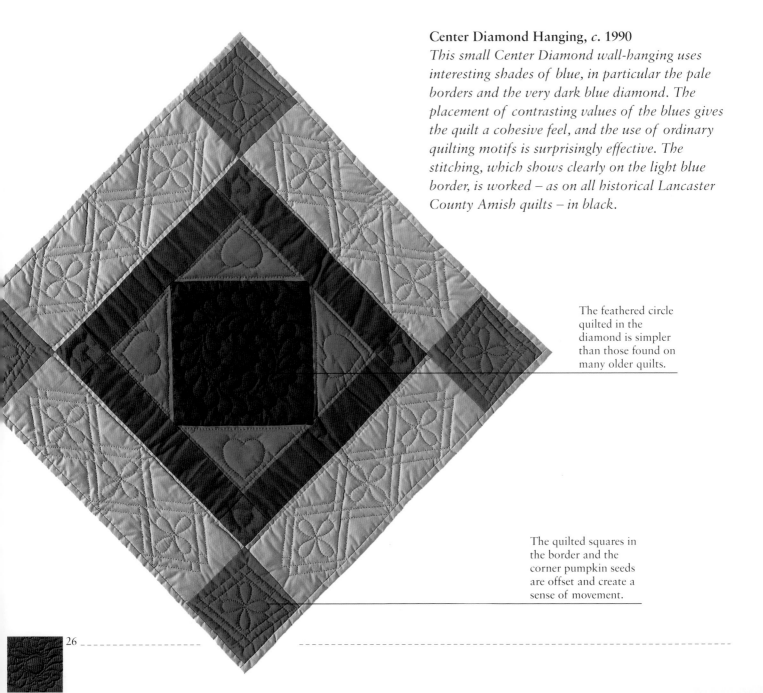

Center Diamond Hanging, *c*. 1990
This small Center Diamond wall-hanging uses interesting shades of blue, in particular the pale borders and the very dark blue diamond. The placement of contrasting values of the blues gives the quilt a cohesive feel, and the use of ordinary quilting motifs is surprisingly effective. The stitching, which shows clearly on the light blue border, is worked – as on all historical Lancaster County Amish quilts – in black.

The feathered circle quilted in the diamond is simpler than those found on many older quilts.

The quilted squares in the border and the corner pumpkin seeds are offset and create a sense of movement.

QUILTING AND PATTERN VARIATIONS

Traditionally, the quilting on this pattern features close rows of crosshatching, especially in the central field, reflecting the simple practicality of the design. The Lancaster County Amish are particularly well respected for their detailed quilting work, and their most elaborate effects occur in the early twentieth-century quilts. More intricate and "worldly" motifs, such as stars and roses, appeared in the 1920s and these embellishments can be seen in Center Diamond quilts of the time.

There are a number of standard variations on the Center Diamond. Its forerunner was the Center Square, typical of the conservative Lancaster County Amish and relying on bold geometric shapes and strong colors for effect.

A popular variation is the Sawtooth Diamond. The edges in this pattern are finished with half blocks to make the effect of a sawtooth, rather than a straight, edge. A Floating Diamond, marked by the absence of corner blocks, is also common. Later variations show the introduction of more complicated

Sawtooth Center Diamond, *c.* 1990
This beautifully executed Sawtooth Center Diamond is an outstanding example of the dramatic effect that can be created by using just two colors. The predominance of straight geometric lines in the quilting motifs reinforces the angularity of the patchwork, while the sharp edges are softened by the clamshells and the rose in the central area.

The border is created without corner squares to achieve an uncluttered look.

The overlapping clamshells in the red diamond lead the eye outward from the rose medallion in the middle.

patterns and more involved quilting effects into the basic Center Diamond; such designs as Sunshine and Shadow or Nine-Patch (see pages 37 and 47) are often used in the diamond.

MEDALLION-STYLE QUILTS

The Center Diamond is an example of a medallion style of quilt. Popular during the early 1800s in America, this style persisted among the Amish when other non-Amish quilters began using new techniques and patterns. The Amish interest in preserving tradition carried through to their quilts and this type of pattern was one that passed on with little change through the generations.

The Center Diamond pattern also closely resembles the decoration found on some examples of early leather-bound prayer books used by the Amish. These books, dating from the late eighteenth century, show a central brass diamond and decorated square corner pieces. These strong, geometric shapes were clearly a familiar style of decoration in the early Amish communities.

Four hearts are joined to create a different pattern.

Center Diamond, *c.* 1890
This woolen quilt is typical of those made at the end of the nineteeth century. Both the top and the backing are wool, while the batting (wadding) is a thin layer of cotton. The stunning quilting is a sampler of recognized designs, including feathers, crosshatching, pumpkin seeds, stars, and hearts – the latter are repeated in each element in turn, from the diamond center to the inner border to the outer one. The unusual colors are highly effective.

The outer border contains a single heart motif.

The wide black binding frames the finished quilt.

The central medallion of the diamond is a feature found in many early quilts and other textiles from all over the world. The design probably developed when needleworkers were searching for a satisfying pattern in which to use geometric shapes. Early English embroidered bedspreads were often worked with a central motif, and in the eighteenth century full-size pieced and appliquéd quilts also used a central medallion. In the early 1800s, specially printed panels were made for use as the central panel in these English quilts. Also called "framed" quilts, these textiles showed a square, diamond, or even oval in the center, surrounded by one or more frames or borders. Although the medallion was typically made using the appliqué technique, patchwork did sometimes make up the borders for the piece.

The medallion style was exported to the American colonies, where quilters copied the needlework of their English mothers, grandmothers, and friends, and eventually the idea of working a center design found its way into Amish quilting.

Center Diamond, *c.* 1990
The use of only two colors on this Center Diamond quilt is as unusual as the quilting motifs chosen. In fact, this quilt needs the more elaborate quilting designs because the very basic piecing would be unremarkable without the texture created by the stitching. The dark binding adds depth to the simple patchwork. Combining two different flowers – chrysanthemums in the central diamond and roses in the outer border – on such a small piece is unconventional.

The straight lines stitched on the outer border intersect to create triangles, which are interrupted by roses.

The feathered circle in the center is repeated in each of the four outer corners.

Religion

*T*HE AMISH PRACTICE *their religion twenty-four hours a day, seven days a week, and their faith informs every action and thought. Their bible-based Christianity is founded on five main principles: the scripture, adult baptism, brotherhood, non-resistance, and separation from the outside world. Adult baptism is a feature which distinguished the Amish's early forerunners, the Anabaptists, from mainstream reformed churches in Europe.*

The Amish consider themselves a church of voluntary believers and believe that joining a church should be a matter of choice, not something forced upon an unknowing infant. An emphasis on brotherhood, looking after each other spiritually, morally, and physically, helps keep the family and community together.

Scripture is the basis of all Amish belief. Biblical teachings are used to explain or emphasize much of the Amish way of life. The Martyrs' Mirror, *a book of inspirational stories of early Anabaptists, and the* Ausbund, *their hymnbook which dates from the sixteenth century, are the Amish's religious books. The* Ordnung, *the rules and regulations that guide everyday Amish life, is oral and unwritten. Some of the rules are based directly on scripture, while others are traditional.*

The Amish belief in separation from the outside world is also scripture based. They frequently quote from Romans 12:2: "And be not conformed to this world." Most aspects of Amish life have developed as protection against the perceived evils of the world.

The Amish faith is practiced plainly, without the ornamentation of many other religions. Their religious hierarchy is as limited and unstructured as possible. Each church district consists of about twenty families and has two elders and a deacon. Four or five districts together have a bishop, who has the highest authority, but neither lives nor dresses differently from the rest of the community. He administers the Amish sacraments of baptism, communion, marriage, and burial. The elders perform the everyday work among the congregation, looking after the members and conducting Sunday service.

The Amish faith is practised simply, without the ornamentation of many other religions.

The process of selecting a new minister is unusual: humility is considered one of the most important virtues, making it impossible to campaign for votes or put oneself forward. The Amish believe no one person is better than any other. A man's behavior throughout his life is of major importance when considering candidates for ordination. All baptized men in the church district are eligible, and the term of service for an elder or bishop is life.

When a new minister is needed, there is a time of preparation when the district members consider the possible choices and the eligible men reflect upon the possible path ahead. All baptized men and women in the congregation then vote for their choice. The men who receive three or more votes proceed to the next stage.

These men wait outside while the bishop slips a bible verse written on a small piece of paper into a waiting pile of hymnbooks. The men file back into the room and choose a book. The one with the slip of paper is the new minister. He is not congratulated but offered commiserations because of the burden of responsibility that now falls on him. This system of election takes the choice out of the hands of the people and into the hands of God.

Religion and prayer are a central part of Amish life.

The Amish do not have church buildings; religious services are conducted in the homes of members of the congregation and occur on alternate Sundays, while private or family prayers are held on the other Sundays.

The living accommodation of an Amish house is designed so that much of the ground floor inter-communicates, allowing the maximum number of people to be seated. Families with small houses hold the service in their barns in the warmer summer months.

Some time is spent preparing the house for the Sunday service. Space is made for the special benches, that will be delivered by wagon on the Friday or Saturday. Chairs are placed at the front for the ministers and the man of the house. The men sit on one side of the room, facing the front, and the women sit on the other. Children always sit with their parents. Illness and emergency are the only acceptable excuses for not attending.

The actual service lasts about three hours and follows a pattern familiar to most church-goers. There are hymns (but no accompanying music), sermons, bible readings, and prayers. The proceedings are conducted in German. The service is attended by two elders, and the man of the house also participates. After the final hymn, announcements are made, then everyone exits quickly so that the benches can be rearranged for lunch.

The meal, prepared by the home family, is simple, often consisting of bread, jam, peanut butter, pickles, relishes, cheese, apple pie, and coffee and tea. Most families stay through the afternoon to socialize.

Sunday services are held in the homes of members of the congregation.

Making the Quilt

THE CENTER DIAMOND QUILT, the quintessential Amish design, is complicated slightly by its long bias seams, which must be sewn carefully to avoid stretching them. However, the heavy quilting traditionally worked on Center Diamond quilts, such as dense areas of crosshatching, eases the impact of any distortion and enhances the bold, simple spaces provided by the design.

CUTTING GUIDE

Piece	Quantity	Measurement
Center squares	1 blue	14½ in (37 cm) square
	1 black	15¼ in (39 cm) square
Inner border	4 green strips	2½ in (6 cm) wide
	4 pink squares	2½ in (6 cm) square
Outer border	4 burgundy strips	7 in (18 cm) wide
	4 black squares	7 in (18 cm) square

See page 126 for the total amount of fabric required to complete this quilt.

CUTTING

1 Cut out the blue center square and the larger black square. To make the four right-angle triangles, cut  the black square in half along the diagonal, then cut the resulting triangles in half again.

2 Following the Cutting Guide *(left)*, use a rotary cutter to cut out the inner and outer border strips, the four black corner squares,  and the pink corner squares.

STITCHING

3 Start stitching the central diamond. Match the center of the long side of a black triangle to the center of each side of the blue square and mark with a pin. Stitch with a ¼-inch (6-mm) seam. *Inset*: Sew opposite sides in turn, pressing the first two sides before adding the remaining two.

4 Add the third and fourth sides to the blue square as in Step 3, then press the finished piece. *Inset*: With a small pair of scissors, trim the overlapping points of black fabric at the corners of the blue square.

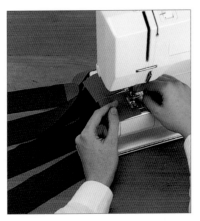

5 To make the inner borders, stitch a pink corner square to the end of each strip. For speed, you can chain-piece *(see page 115)* all four strips at once.

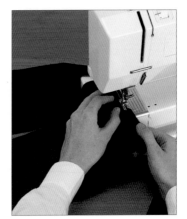

6 Following the method used in Step 5, chain-piece the outer border squares to the outer strips. Press the seams to one side.

7 Apply one inner border strip to the pieced center square, right sides together. The corner square should overhang the top edge of the center section. Begin stitching approximately 3 inches (7.5 cm) below the corner square with a 1/4-inch (6-mm) seam.

8 Add the second and third strips and stitch in place, matching the seams precisely where the corner squares meet the center section.

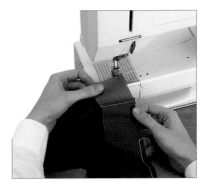

9 Stitch the fourth border in place, then return to the overhanging corner square on the first border and finish stitching the seam.

10 Add the outer border strips following the method used for the inner strips in Steps 7 to 9. Make sure the inner edges match.

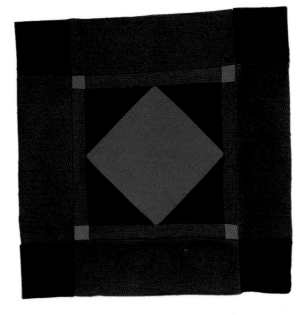

11 Once the outer borders have been added, press all the seams to one side, working on the wrong side of the quilt. The finished piece is ready to be marked with quilting patterns.

MARKING

12 Using the heart motif on page 123, mark the hearts on the center, the outer border squares, and the inner pink squares.

13 Once you have traced one heart, cut the template down to the next marked line and mark around the smaller heart.

14 The diagram above shows the position of the cross-hatching and the simple cable pattern used on the inner border strip *(see page 124)*.

15 Add the backing and batting, and baste (tack) the layers together following the instructions on page 117. Follow the marked patterns and quilt by hand, using quilting thread. When all the quilting is complete, remove the basting threads and bind the quilt *(see page 117)*.

MEASUREMENT GUIDE

MAKING A CENTER DIAMOND QUILT IN A DIFFERENT SIZE

The quilt from this project can be used as a crib quilt. Because the center diamond is a square design, it does not work well on a single (twin) bed. For a double (full) or kingsize bed, you can add a larger top border to extend the quilt. You can change the size of the finished quilt by simply enlarging the width of the outer border.

	Center diamond	Inner border/squares	Outer border/squares	Setting triangles	Top border
Double (full)	30 in (76 cm)	4 in (10 cm)	18 in (46 cm)	20 in (51 cm)	36 in (91 cm)
Queen/King	40 in (102 cm)	4 1/2 in (11.5 cm)	15 in (38 cm)	32 in (81 cm)	32 in (81 cm)

Sunshine and Shadow

❖❖❖❖❖❖❖❖❖❖❖❖❖❖❖❖❖❖❖❖❖

HE SUNSHINE AND SHADOW pattern is an outstanding example of Amish creativity. The echoing shades of light and dark create a dramatic and vibrant design, contained within broad, solid borders, that may come as a surprise if one expects muted or quiet quilts from the Amish.

Most examples date from the early twentieth century. The pattern developed from earlier basic patchworks, such as the Hexagon or the One-Patch, which were pieced randomly. The Sunshine and Shadow needs careful color placement. Twentieth-century Amish quilters began to experiment with color, encouraged by the increased choice of hues available through new manufacturing processes. By the 1930s, Amish quilts were frequently decorative, richly colored, with intricate patchwork.

Sunshine and Shadow, *c.* 1940
Seventeen colors provide the darks and the lights of this quintessential quilt. The contrast between the lines of color creates a strong secondary diamond shape.

The Sunshine and Shadow quilt can be seen as a symbol for what it is to be Amish. The color scraps symbolize plainness and frugality, but the overall exuberance of the finished quilt reflects the joy of their lives and close-knit families and communities; the wide borders symbolize their strong beliefs. The name of the quilt also exemplifies the Amish attitude to life: along with light, there is darkness; along with joy, sorrow.

JUXTAPOSITIONING OF COLOR

The pattern is made up of small fabric scraps arranged so that they reflect light and dark alternately. Of all the Amish quilts, it is the one most obviously a "scrap" quilt, using much smaller pieces of fabric compared to the early traditional designs, such as the Bars.

The Amish quilters have an amazing ability to compose wonderful color combinations. Although the colors are often dark, they are

The tiny bright pink square at each corner holds the whole design together and contrasts strikingly with the color of the inner border.

Sunshine and Shadow, c. 1990
The graded shades of purple, blue, red, and green used here are typical. A strong black border encloses and holds together the vibrant colors of this quilt, and the single line of the palest shade gives the entire piece a lift. The quilting on a typical Sunshine and Shadow is generally simple crosshatching on the colored blocks, with more elaborate quilting on the borders.

The corner of the inner border is quilted with an unusual leaf.

The feathered cable on the outer border meets in the center of each side.

rich. Muted and deeper shades of colors are used among the more conservative Amish communities; if bright colors are used, they are counter-balanced by more natural hues.

The manipulation of color reaches its apex in the Sunshine and Shadow quilt. Careful choice of color is essential when preparing the quilt, and the women sometimes spend weeks planning the composition before any sewing takes place. Some shades will produce soft, quiet quilts while others will make a quilt that is strikingly vivid. Generally, the smaller the blocks and the more colors used, the more complex and interesting the design, though beautiful and effective quilts have been made using larger blocks and as few as three different colors. A non-Amish version of Sunshine and Shadow, called Trip Around the World, is arranged in the same way but relies less on the light/dark shading of colors.

Sunshine and Shadow,
c. **1990**
This small wall-hanging is a typical scrap Sunshine and Shadow, but it is surprising because the fabrics used are synthetic. Some of the squares, made from a kind of nylon knit, have a slight rib that creates a secondary texture. The rather lurid colors are typical of this type of man-made fiber, which is used widely by the Amish because it is inexpensive and easy to launder.

The backing of pure cotton is brought around the outer edges to create the binding.

The central quilting is derived from straight lines that follow the diagonal of each square to create a diamond pattern.

QUILTING EFFECTS

Because of the tiny patches of colored fabric, elaborate quilting is confined to the wide borders. Crosshatching, to secure the top, batting (wadding), and backing together, is done on the center patchwork of the quilt.

When applied to the large expanses of fabric in the quilt, Amish quilting is soft and rounded to contrast with the straight geometric shapes of patchwork sections. Typical quilting patterns are flowing ones, such as feathers, scrolls, wreaths, and cables, and ones that recall the Swiss and German origins of the Amish, such as hearts, stars, and flowers. Other motifs are based on simple geometric shapes, such as triangles, concentric circles, and lines.

Motifs were transferred using templates made of card or tin, many of which have been passed down the generations. Experienced quilters may even draw the motifs freehand.

The pattern is produced by using just three shades of each color and repeating them as the work moves outward.

The pansies quilted on the border are unorthodox.

Sunshine and Shadow, c. 1990
The colors of all Sunshine and Shadow quilts are, of course, graded, but in this example, the color families are kept together more rigidly than is usual. The colors themselves are slightly stronger and more unconventional, especially the combination of brown and purple; and the red corner squares neatly echo the darkest red from the center. The rectangular shape is also unusual.

Farming

FAMILY, FAITH, and the farm are the cornerstones of Amish life. The Amish choose the rural lifestyle as one that enables self-sufficiency and separation. The farm is considered the best place to raise children and teach them the value of honest hard work. To own a farm and work it is every Amish boy's dream. In the simple ways of the Old Order Amish, he is destined to till the soil, live closely with his animals, breathe the fresh air, and avoid the temptations of the cities.

Most Amish still live on a farm, although it is no longer possible to provide every newly married couple with land. In Lancaster County this amazingly fertile farmland is the most expensive Amish-owned land in the United States, of interest to industry and tourism in the nearby state of New York, and in Washington and Philadelphia.

Despite changes on the farm, day-to-day life remains the same for most Amish people.

Self-sufficiency is the cornerstone of independence, and farms and gardens provide for the basic needs of the community. Commercial crops, such as tobacco and corn, are grown and dairy farms provide milk, butter, and cheese. At harvest time the whole community, including the children, will lend a hand.

The Amish rely on horse power to work the land.

Horses or mules are used for field work. Tractor engines may be used on the farm for turning machinery, although modern tractors are rarely used themselves as they are associated with cars.

Other changes have occurred over the years. In the 1950s mechanical milking machines and mechanical hay balers were permitted. By the 1960s some farmers had generators in order to run their welding machines, especially useful to repair and maintain the often antique farm equipment or to adapt new machinery to horse power. In the 1970s pneumatic and hydraulic power began appearing on the farm and in the workshop.

Despite these changes on the farm, day-to-day life for most Amish people remains the same as it has been for many years, with the majority of Amish still living and working away from the hustle and bustle of modern life.

Making the Quilt

*S*UNSHINE AND SHADOW CAN BE assembled by cutting squares and sewing them together one by one by hand or machine, or you can use this ingenious strip-piecing method that relies on accurate rotary cutting. If you cut 4-inch (10-cm) strips, you can double the size of the finished quilt to make it suitable for a double bed.

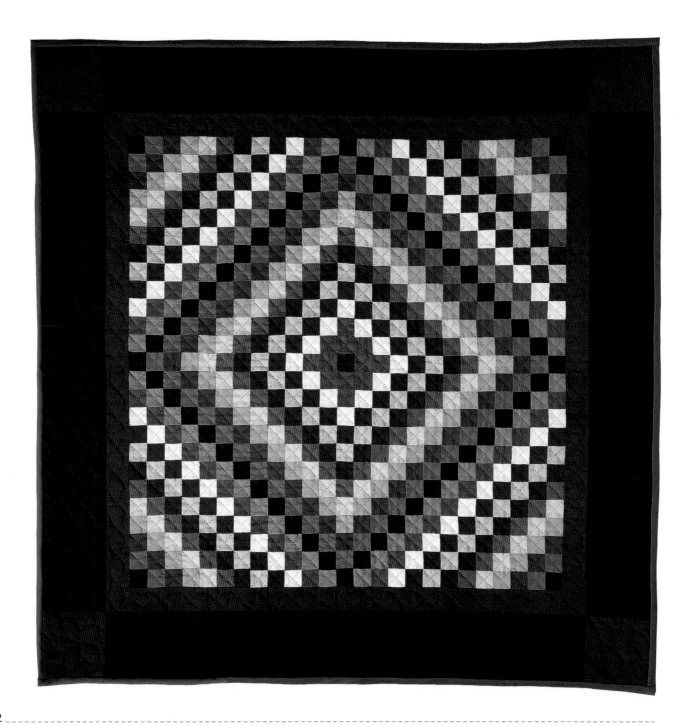

CUTTING GUIDE

Piece	Quantity	Measurement
Strips	3 of colors 1–12	2 in (5 cm)
	1 of color 13	2 in (5 cm)
Center square	1 color 14	2 in (5 cm) square
Border strips	4 purple	2½ in (6 cm)
	4 green	6 in (15 cm)
Border squares	4 purple	6 in (15 cm) square

See page 126 for the total amount of fabric required to complete this quilt.

CUTTING

1 Following the Cutting Guide *(left)*, cut out the strips of different colors and cut the border strips and corner squares. *Inset:* Lay out the strips in order.

STITCHING

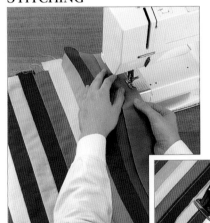

2 Place color 1 on color 2, right sides together, and stitch with a ¼-inch (6-mm) seam. Place color 3 on color 2, and stitch from the bottom. Repeat to join all colors in sequence 1–12, alternating the stitching direction to prevent the fabric from arcing. Repeat to produce three finished sets of strips. *Inset:* Press the seams to one side.

3 Join color 1 to color 12 on one set of strips. Repeat for each set to make three tubes of pieced fabric.

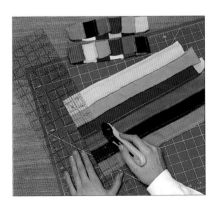

4 Cut across the tube, along the straight grain, to make rings 2 inches (5 cm) wide. Cut 48 rings in total, leaving about half of the third tube: set it aside for use in Step 7.

5 Unpick the seam of one ring between colors 1 and 12 (refer to Step 1 to check the color sequence). Unpick the seam of a second ring between color 2 and color 1.

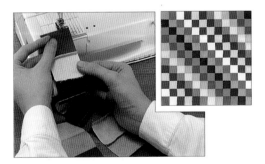

6 Place the strip starting with color 1 on that starting with color 2 and stitch them with a ¼-inch (6-mm) seam. Continue unpicking color by color; add each strip in turn. *Inset:* Make four identical blocks.

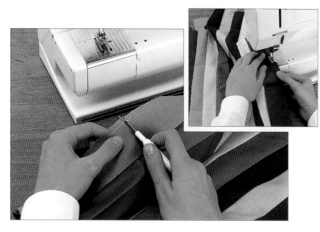

7 Using the uncut tube from Step 4, unpick the seam between colors 11 and 12, then unpick color 12 and remove the strip. *Inset:* Stitch color 13 to color 1.

8 Using the block from Step 7, cut four 2-inch (5-cm) strips. Stitch the square of color 14 – the central square – to color 13 on the end of one of the strips.

9 Lay out the four large pieced squares so that color 1 meets in the center and color 11 appears at each of the four outer corners.

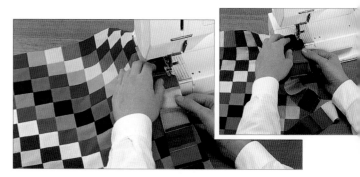

10 Stitch one strip from Step 8 to one side of a pieced square with color 13 adjacent to color 1. Repeat to make three identical pieces. *Inset:* Stitch the final strip with the center square to the side of one of these blocks, with the center square adjacent to color 13.

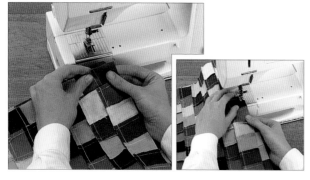

11 Join the second large square to that with the center square to make half of the finished block. *Inset:* Join the large square without the color 13 strip to the third square, with color 13 adjacent to color 1 on each side.

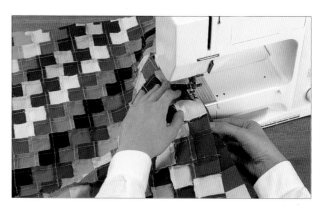

12 Join the two halves, matching the seams carefully. Check the layout carefully before you stitch.

13 Start to add the borders. Add the inner borders to the completed square by stitching a 2¹/2-inch (6-cm) strip of purple to two opposite sides, then trim the edges. *Inset:* Add the remaining two sides.

14 Chain-piece *(see page 115)* the corner squares to the outer border strips and press the seams.

15 Align the top of one strip to one corner of the quilt with the corner square overhanging. Start stitching about 8 inches (20 cm) below the corner using a ¹/4-inch (6 mm) seam. Join the three remaining strips in turn. *Inset:* When the fourth strip is in position, stitch the overhanging corner in place.

MARKING

16 Mark the quilting for the borders using the motifs on pages 124–25. Add the batting and backing *(see page 116)* and work the quilting. To finish the quilt, trim and bind the edges *(see page 117)*.

17 To mark the crosshatching, use a strip of ¹/4-inch (6-mm) masking tape along each diagonal of each square. Quilt each line separately before marking the next.

Nine-Patch

❖❖❖❖❖❖❖❖❖❖❖

AS AMISH WOMEN BEGAN to be influenced by their non-Amish neighbors, their patchwork gradually moved away from rigid geometric shapes. Different techniques were traded back and forth among early Americans, and as the early block patchwork ideas spread, the Nine-Patch pattern made its way into Amish workrooms.

Squares are the fundamental patchwork unit and easy to multiply to form different designs, so the development of four- and nine-patch blocks came early on in American patchwork history. One of the first examples of a Nine-Patch pattern is an antique 21-inch (53-cm) square bag, dated May 22, 1836, used for holding paper for an outhouse (privy).

PATTERN VARIATIONS

Four- and nine-patch are the most basic units of block composition and can be cut and varied according to the scale and color of the finished piece.

Double Nine-Patch, *c.* 1930
The random placement of colors in this amazing Amish scrap quilt, filled with sparkling detail and intricate quilting, gives the piece movement and energy.

These patterns rely on variations of shading and color for their overall effect. The Nine-Patch block is the foundation of many other patchwork patterns, including Ohio Star, Turkey Tracks, Monkey Wrench, and Jacob's Ladder. There is virtually an unending list of Nine-Patch derivations. The Double Nine-Patch, so called because nine squares make up several – usually five – of the nine patches in a block, is perhaps the most striking because of the variations of color that are possible when designing it.

The Nine-Patch quilt is made by dividing the basic blocks into nine equal squares or into double nine-patches. The basic nine-patch blocks can be placed on the final quilt top in a horizontal plane or on point. They can also be tightly grouped or divided by sashing.

Often nine-patches, whether double or single, will alternate with solid blocks. Usually an equal number of blocks will be used horizontally and vertically to make up a square quilt; this is especially a feature of a Lancaster County quilt. Nine-Patches from other Amish

The "cup" design on the inner border is marked using the rim of a cup or glass.

Nine-Patch, *c*. 1950
This small Nine-Patch quilt is made in typical Lancaster County Amish colors and form. The defining feature is the use of the same fabric for the background squares and the outer square of the nine-patch blocks, which creates a cross effect instead of the expected squared-off nine-patch. The blocks are all set on point and quilted across the seams to create secondary squares.

The straight lines of stitching on the outer border are set slightly on the diagonal from the corners and meet in the middle, forming a V shape.

communities are often made up to create rectangular quilts. Four- and Nine-Patch variations were the only patterns permitted by the Nebraskan Amish, who followed very strict limitations in their quiltmaking, but these two patterns were also very popular among the Amish communities in Ohio and Indiana.

COMPOSITION AND COLOR

Although the basic idea of the Nine-Patch is simple, the use of light and dark colors create different areas of interest in a piece of work.

An emphasis on light colors in a particular block makes that section of the block leap out of the overall design; conversely, an emphasis on darks makes that section recede, or merge, into the background. With all the different possible uses of tone and color, the creation of a Nine-Patch can be a challenging and interesting undertaking.

The size of the blocks and the positioning of the blocks within the quilt can also be manipulated for effect. Many of the most surprising and impressive results occur spontaneously

Double Nine-Patch, *c.* 1990
This modern Nine-Patch retains all the beauty of a time-honored nineteenth-century quilt. The randomly placed scraps move around the surface, and the lighter colors punctuate the design. Elaborate and beautifully stitched quilting vies for attention and threatens to overwhelm the simplicity of the double nine-patch blocks.

The feather quilting on the outer border flows uninterrupted through the corner squares, but stops in the center of each side, where a flower appears.

Because the double nine-patch blocks are placed on point, the crosshatching appears as a grid.

Amish Clothing

HE AMISH ARE often called the "plain people" because of their plain, dark-colored, modest garments and fabrics. The traditional style of clothing prevents the Amish from dressing for enhancement, fashion, or pride. It keeps the community equal; no one can show off his or her new clothes and no one is tempted to waste money on adornment.

The women wear dresses in a number of different colors, but always in plain, never patterned, fabrics. The dress is made to the same design: a shirtwaist with a waistband and loosely gathered skirt, over which is worn a black apron and cape, giving the woman a very somber appearance. Among the Old Order Amish, the dress, apron, and cape are fastened with straight or dress-making pins instead of buttons, which are considered worldly and fancy.

Amish men wear black trousers and jackets with shirts in solid colors. The trousers are not tailored to fit, but are often baggy and held up by suspenders (braces). They have a large sailor-type flap which gives them their name of "broadfall trousers." A black hat is worn in the winter and a straw one in summer.

An Amish woman's hair is never cut, but is parted in the middle and pulled

Amish clothing has changed little throughout the generations.

tightly back into a knot at the nape of the neck. A white organdy prayer covering is worn over the hair at all times. A black bonnet may also be worn in bad weather.

The man's hair is cut at home and tends to be bowl- or pudding-basin shaped for ease and practicality. He is clean shaven until his wedding day, and from then on he grows a full beard. The upper lip continues to be shaved, however, as the Amish believe moustaches are proud and fancy, and have military connotations.

Amish clothing has changed little throughout the generations. A new invention or change is discussed in the church district. The new trend is put on trial and the effects observed. If the change, and it could be something as small as the shape of the prayer covering, does not interfere with Amish faith or life, it is accepted.

Traditional style dresses are made in subtle colors.

without regard for color placement. Although most Amish quilts were planned to some extent, the chance of unexpected effects was more likely when making the Nine-Patch or Double Nine-Patch. Each single block can be quite different, and the overall effect not evident until the quilt is completed.

A Double Nine-Patch quilt made of many small pieces is given life and vibrancy from its varying colors. Although most Lancaster County quilts use a large amount of dark blue,

the small pieces can be in many colors, light and dark. Children's dresses and shirts are plain, light colors. The scraps available from children's clothing range from white, through pale blue and pink to green, purple, and black.

The Nine-Patch is a good example of how the Amish are able to create a work of art out of very ordinary scraps. In their simplicity of design and astonishing use of color, the quilts could be mistaken for sophisticated works of modern art.

The double cables on the outer border are stopped at the corners by six-point stars.

Crib quilt, *c.* 1990
This simple piece in two dark colors – green and blue – typifies a functional Amish crib quilt. It consists of six nine-patch blocks separated by sashing in the same color as the background squares. The quilting is somewhat irregular, as befits a quilt made to be used, not for show or sale. Despite its obvious practicality, it has great charm.

Making the Quilt

HIS SMALL NINE-PATCH RUNNER with its jewel colors on black could be expanded into a charming crib quilt by making more blocks; for example, three across and five down. To make a bed quilt, increase the size of the finished blocks to 12 or 15 inches (30.5 or 38 cm).

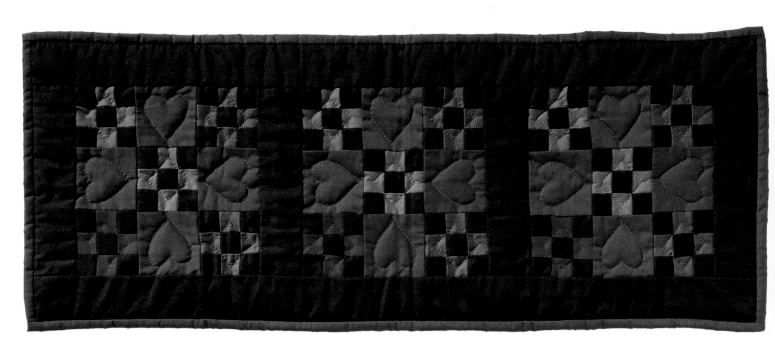

CUTTING GUIDE

Piece	Quantity	Measurement
Squares	12 dark blue	3¹/₂ in (9 cm)
Strips (A)	1 green, purple, red, light blue, turquoise	1¹/₂ x 18 in (4 x 46 cm)
Strips (B)	3 black	1¹/₂ in (4 cm)
Sashing strips	4 black	2¹/₂ x 9¹/₄ in (6 x 23.5 cm)
	2 black	2¹/₂ x 34¹/₂ in (6 x 88 cm)

See page 126 for the total amount of fabric required to complete this quilt.

CUTTING

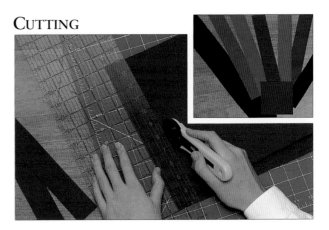

1 The narrow strips are used to make the small nine-patch blocks. Following the instructions given in the Cutting Guide (left), cut one strip of each colored fabric and three in black, using a rotary cutter, ruler, and cutting mat (see inset). Cut out the blue squares.

STITCHING

2 Stitch the strips together in two configurations for each of the colors: A/B/A and B/A/B. *Inset:* Press all the seams to one side.

3 Cut each of the strips into 1¹/₂-inch (4-cm) wide units. For each block you will need two strips of configuration A/B/A and one of B/A/B.

4 Stitch the pieced units into nine-patch blocks; you can chain-piece for speed *(see page 115)*. Make three blocks of each color.

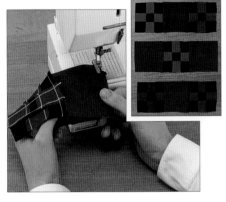

5 Combine the plain dark blue squares with the pieced blocks into three strips *(see inset)*. Join the strips together to create a block.

6 Apply the sashing strips to one side of each block. Stitch the blocks together in a row and add the fourth sashing strip to the end.

7 Add one long border strip along each side of the finished piece.

MARKING

8 Using the heart and diamond templates on page 123, mark the motifs clearly with an appropriate marker that will show against the dark material.

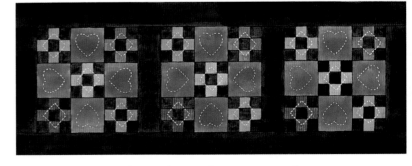

9 The diagram above shows the position of the quilting motifs. Add the batting and backing *(see page 116)* and work the quilting by hand, then bind the edges *(see page 117)*.

Shoo-fly

❖❖❖❖❖❖❖❖❖❖❖❖❖❖❖❖❖❖

A SIMPLE NINE-PATCH variation, the Shoo-fly is very effective when made up using just two colors, but experiments with a number of colors can also be successful. Although it is not as popular as some other Nine-Patch variations, the pattern makes a very attractive quilt. It can also appear as a scrap quilt, with each block done in different colors. In plain Amish fabrics this random use of color creates surprising effects. The design requires just five square blocks and four blocks halved to form triangles, so it makes an excellent starter block; a cushion or small wall-hanging can be made in a day.

Many different compositions are effective, and the blocks can be separated by sashing in a contrasting color, or the blocks can alternate with solid quilted blocks. Although the Shoo-fly lends itself well to classic Amish colors, such as red and black, it can make an interesting scrap quilt when done in patterned fabrics separated by plain sashing, with each block taking on a different look.

The finished quilt is quilted simply with the heaviest stitching on the borders. The Shoo-fly patches can be quilted around their outline, with a small symbol, perhaps a heart, in the center of each block.

Shoo-fly, 1997
This Shoo-fly wall-hanging illustrates the different shapes and effects that can be achieved by varying the placement of colors within the shoo-fly block.

THE ORIGIN OF THE NAME

This pattern is also called the Fence Row, but is most often referred to as the Shoo-fly. In Lancaster County, the Pennsylvania Dutch make a dessert of the same name. The dessert is a molasses pie and the measure of quality is based on how sticky the pie is. The name of the pie comes from the need, when cooling the desserts on the windowsill, to keep shooing the

flies away. Because this dish is such an integral part of Lancaster County lives, most people believe the quilting pattern has some connection with this pastry.

Although the Shoo-fly pattern was made in Lancaster County in earlier years, it rarely appears there today and the pattern is essentially a Midwest design. It is most likely that the name Shoo-fly comes from the Shoo-fly

The double bindings in mauve and black are an unusual feature.

Shoo-fly, c. 1990
This classic wall-hanging, with all the blocks in just two colors, is Shoo-fly as it would have appeared throughout the generations. The plain squares provide a background for fine quilting, while the inner and outer borders and the contrasting binding lift the piece out of the ordinary.

The crosshatching continues across both borders, creating a simple zigzag line on the inner one.

plant (*Nicandra*). This plant has four bell-shaped, violet-blue flowers branching from one central stem, and probably inspired the four colored corners of the patchwork block.

Along with the Monkey Wrench and its variation, the Churn Dash, the Shoo-fly pattern is commonly found among the most conservative Amish groups in Ohio, where it is usually completed in blues, reds, and blacks.

Black is, however, a color rarely found in Lancaster County quilts. Numerous examples of the Shoo-fly can also be found in Indiana and Iowa.

Much of the attraction of the Shoo-fly is its simplicity. It appeals to patchworkers of all abilities because it is easily pieced, but imaginative manipulations of the blocks can produce intricate and sophisticated results.

Shoo-fly, 1900

This is a wonderful example of a scrap quilt. The muted colors are typical of nineteenth-century Amish patchwork, and they produce a subtle effect throughout the entire quilt. While most of the blocks are made in two colors, those devised from three or more are obviously using up available scraps. Particularly interesting are the top and bottom right-hand blocks, which give an entirely different shape to the shoo-fly design. The blocks are all set on point, and the crosshatching is done as a squared grid covering the entire surface.

The quadruple cable pattern continues from the outer border onto the inner one.

The top and bottom borders are wider than the side borders, perhaps to make the quilt fit a particular bed.

Amish Symbolism

AMISH CLOTHING, *the horse and buggy, and the form of language are just some of the many signs and symbols that set the Amish apart from their neighbors, and which translate into guidelines for conformity within the group. In a world where language is frugal and sparse, actions and visible outward signs take on great significance.*

Amish dress sets the plain people apart from the world while enabling them to disappear within their own group. Individuality and vanity are out of place in an Amish community and the Amish people's attire are as plain as their houses. Variations of dress signify important differences among the Amish, such as marital status, age, and standing in the community, although outsiders may not notice or recognize these subtleties.

The original Amish settlers spoke Swiss-German and a dialect of that language is spoken by the Amish today. Amish people can effectively cut themselves off from "English" neighbors and strangers simply by speaking their own language. Conversation is usually very matter-of-fact and without any of the polite niceties or exuberances used in the outside world. Even a husband and wife do not exchange little words like "thank you," but expect their actions to show how they feel.

One of the best-known symbols of the Amish is the horse and buggy. It is also the most poignant, since its existence proves that the Amish have not sold out to the pressures of the world around them. The horse embodies much that is Amish – an adherence to tradition, slow living, limited amenities, and the willingness to sacrifice modern conveniences and technology. Although the horse and buggy is a symbol that distinguishes the Amish from outsiders, it can also distinguish between different Amish

In a world where language is frugal, actions and visible outward signs take on great significance.

groups. The style of buggy, whether black-, yellow-, or white-topped, open- or closed-top, and other such details, varies according to region or church ordinance.

Because the Amish man can only travel about twenty-five miles per day, his world is small, thus his local area is of prime importance and his sense of community strong. Although the Amish feel there is nothing intrinsically sinful about the car, they feel that it will

Dressing uniformly discourages individuality and vanity.

bring the desire to drive distances and perhaps move away. Owning a car may disperse the family and cause a break down of the community.

The rejection of speed is also part of the reason for the use of the horse and buggy. Many Amish do not ride horses or bicycles because both are considered "fast," in the sense of speed and in terms of showing off. Peace, simplicity, and humility remain the most sought after virtues, and fast cars signify fast, worldly living.

The horse and buggy is a classic symbol of the Amish's rejection of modern life.

Sometimes, however, the Amish do bend the rules. Some non-Amish earn a living driving groups of Amish to weddings, fairs, family reunions, exhibitions, and other events. The Amish are also happy to use public transportation, such as buses and trains, but are not permitted to travel by plane. Interestingly, almost the first thing an Amish person does if he leaves the religion is to buy a car.

Pictorial representation is evident in modern Amish homes, but strictly limited. In Exodus 20: 4-5, the quote "Thou shall not make for yourself a graven image or a likeness of anything" is taken literally. The Amish interpret this as meaning that any image of themselves would be a graven one and therefore unlawful. Amish dolls are made with blank faces – the Amish child's imagination

The horse and buggy is one of the most poignant symbols of Amish beliefs.

supplies the features. Although the Amish are traditionally discouraged from representational art, today there are some Amish artists and woodcarvers. Children are certainly encouraged to draw or paint what they see around them, especially from nature.

The Amish people are very reluctant to be photographed, as posing for photographs shows personal pride and vanity. The Amish feel that the outside world's idol is the "self" and are more interested in the inner person. However, a photograph taken without the Amish person's awareness is not a sin or transgression. Amish children, who have not yet been baptized, may be more freely photographed. As an Amish man said, "We believe that letting ourselves get involved in the world of photography leads us away from, not toward, humility."

Making the Quilt

THIS SMALL QUILT, MADE UP of squares and right-angle triangles in two contrasting colors, is the perfect size for a baby's crib. Since only small pieces of the contrasting fabric are needed, it works well as a scrap quilt, and the pattern is also effective when only one contrasting color is used throughout. It makes an ideal pattern for the beginner. To make a bed quilt, increase the number of Shoo-fly blocks: perhaps 24 for a single bed and 36 for a double.

CUTTING GUIDE

Piece	Quantity	Measurement
Squares for each block	2 from each contrasting color and 2 from background color	5 in (13 cm) square
	4 from background fabric and 1 from contrasting color	4¹/2 in (11.5 cm) square
Sashing and border	navy strips	3¹/2 in (9 cm) wide
	4 salmon squares	3¹/2 in (9 cm)
Outer border	turquoise strips	4¹/2 in (11.5 cm) wide
	4 purple squares	4¹/2 in (11.5 cm)

See page 126 for the total amount of fabric required.

CUTTING

1 Following the Cutting Guide *(left)*, use a rotary cutter, ruler, and mat to cut out the squares for each block from the contrasting colors and background color (turquoise). *Inset:* Cut out the fabric required for the sashing and borders.

STITCHING

2 Place one 5-inch (13-cm) square of each color right sides together. Draw a line across one diagonal on the wrong side of one square and using the line as a guide, stitch a ¹/4-inch (6-mm) seam on each side of the line.

3 Using a rotary cutter, cut along the diagonal line between the seams through both layers, to create two right-angle triangle squares. *Inset*: Press the seams to one side.

4 Before stitching, lay out the squares to check their position *(left)*. To make each nine-patch block, stitch two strips with triangle squares (A) to one background square (B) and one strip of background square (B) stitched to two opposite sides of a plain contrasting square (C).

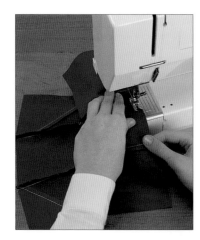

5 Sew the three strips together, matching ¼-inch (6-mm) seams carefully and positioning the triangles correctly. Then press the seams to one side.

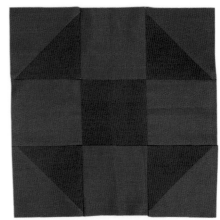

6 The shoo-fly block is now complete. Repeat to make five more blocks in the same way, using the other five colors.

7 Join two blocks into a pair with a vertical strip of sashing, taking a ¼-inch (6-mm) seam. Repeat to make three strips of two blocks plus sashing. Trim the ends of the sashing if necessary.

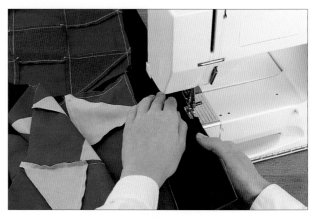

8 Then join the three paired units together horizontally using a long strip of sashing, taking ¼-inch (6-mm) seams.

9 Next, add the pink corner squares to the inner border strips. You can chain-piece for speed (see page 115).

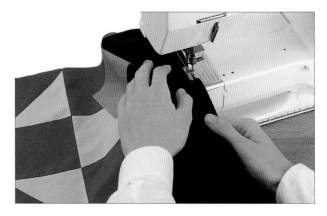

10 Sew the inner borders to the finished center piece. Start stitching approximately 5 inches (13 cm) from the end, with the corner square overhanging the top edge of the finished piece.

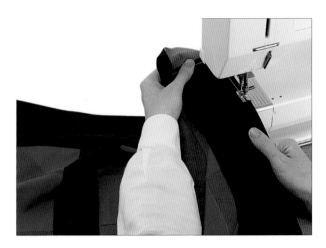

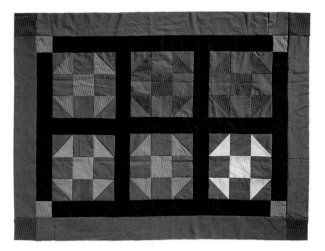

11 Add the fourth border, then return to the overhanging corner square on the first border and finish stitching the seam.

12 Next, add the outer border following Steps 9 to 11, to complete the quilt. Press all the seams. The quilt top is now ready for marking the quilting pattern.

MARKING

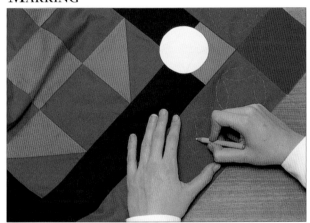

13 To mark the pumpkin seed pattern on the outer border, use the motif on page 124 and trace around it using an appropriate marker. Draw the inner details freehand, matching the points of the "seeds" on each circle.

14 The quilt is simply quilted, with a pumpkin-seed pattern on the outer border and outline quilting on the contrasting colors.

15 Add the batting and backing *(see page 116)* and stitch the quilting patterns by hand. Add the binding *(see page 117)*.

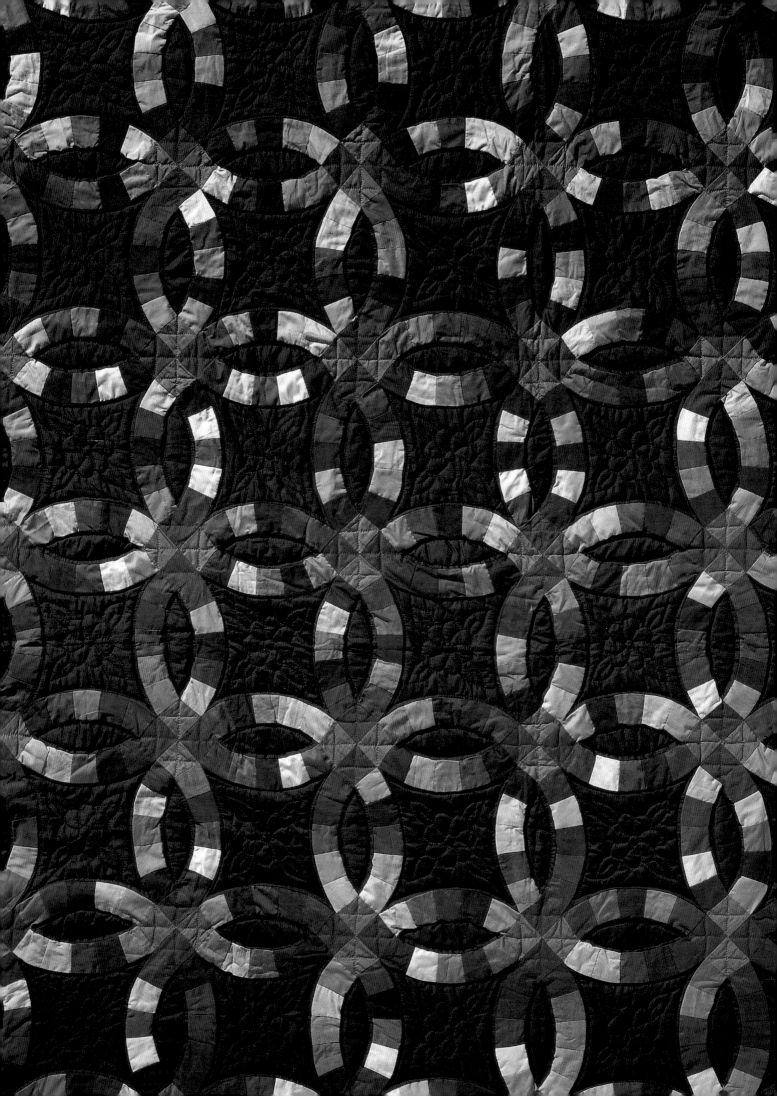

Double Wedding Ring

❖✦❖✦❖✦❖✦❖✦❖✦❖✦❖✦❖✦❖✦❖✦❖✦❖

EVELOPED BY American patchworkers in the early twentieth century, the Double Wedding Ring fits perfectly into the trend to lighter, brighter colors and more elaborate designs that began in the 1920s and 30s. Patchwork in which the lines are curved is an unusual feature in Amish quilts, as their tradition is strongly angular and geometric, using triangles, squares, and diamonds.

The Double Wedding Ring quilt has long been loved by American quiltmakers because of the large number of pieces used and the difficulty of the patchwork. Because the patches are curved and require precision in cutting and piecing, the quilt is a challenge to all patchworkers, and it may be that this challenge is what attracted Amish quilters to the design in the twentieth century. Some American quilts were called

Double Wedding Ring, c. 1990
An Amish Double Wedding Ring has a very different impact from a pretty "worldly" one. When set on a dark background, the jewel-like plain colors seem to shimmer.

"show off" quilts because they involved such intricate piecing. As a reaction against this more "prideful" aspect to quilting, the Amish tended to discourage their women from intricately pieced works, so the Double Wedding Ring is not a typically Amish pattern. Most Amish examples of the Double Wedding Ring quilt date from the 1930s on.

QUILT COLORS

When worked in Amish colors, the Double Wedding Ring is spectacular. It usually incorporates a dark blue or black background, with highly contrasting colors in solid fabrics

making up the rings. Non-Amish versions are often seen in pretty printed pastels on a white or cream background, but they can seem rather bland compared with the depth and character in an Amish version. Unfortunately the quilt is now rarely seen in the Amish interpretation of solid reds, greens, and blues – colors that make it particularly striking and unusual.

Although the quilt's colors are usually chosen to allow the background color to recede and the interlocking rings to stand out, interesting effects can be achieved by varying the color to allow the spaces, rather than the rings, to stand out. The rings can be perfectly circular

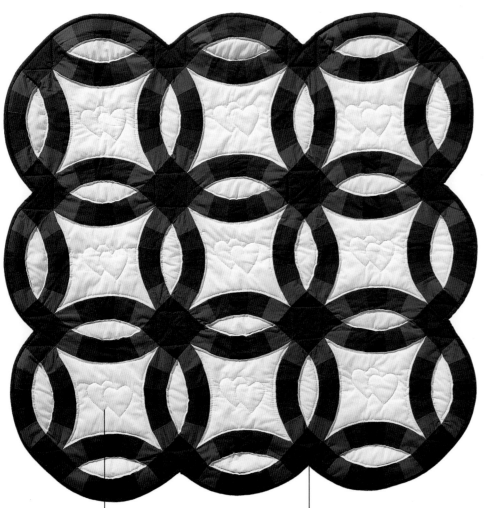

**Double Wedding Ring,
c. 1990**
An up-to-date version of the Amish Double Wedding Ring combines rich colors in the rings with a light background, making this throw more appealing to modern tastes, but keeping the scrap tradition intact. The quilting, as on most Double Wedding Ring quilts, is kept simple. The rings are outlined with stitching, and the centers allow a small motif to be used. The naturally scalloped edges provide another attractive feature.

The double heart motif is in keeping with the wedding theme.

The binding is made from the same fabric as the connecting squares.

but are also seen slightly squared, which alters the overall composition of the piece.

AMISH WEDDING QUILTS

The name of the quilt has no real significance for Amish women, since they do not wear wedding rings, and the quilt itself is not a traditional wedding quilt pattern for the Amish. A Friendship Quilt, made up of individual blocks signed by the makers, is frequently sewn for an Amish wedding celebration instead. Although an especially beautiful quilt will be made for the bridal couple as their "best" quilt, no particular quilt top design or pattern of

quilting is specifically chosen to commemorate the marriage.

Traditionally a number of quilts were sewn in preparation for a marriage – usually five quilts for girls and two for boys – including workaday as well as fancy ones. Quilts included in the dowry may have been made by the bride herself when she was a child – perhaps her first Four-Patch or Nine-Patch. Others include heirloom quilts passed down through generations or those made by friends and family over the years. Special quilting parties, attended by family and friends, are held for teenage girls in order to make their marriage quilts.

**Double Wedding Ring,
c. 1935**
This quilt comes from the heyday of the Double Wedding Ring pattern, although the colors are slightly softer than those used traditionally. As with most older Amish quilts, the patchwork is made of scraps, and each piece in the rings is very small. The black connecting squares and the cream-colored "melons" are both unusual. The edges are contained by the black and the blue outer borders; the scallops created by the rings would be considered worldly if they were not enclosed.

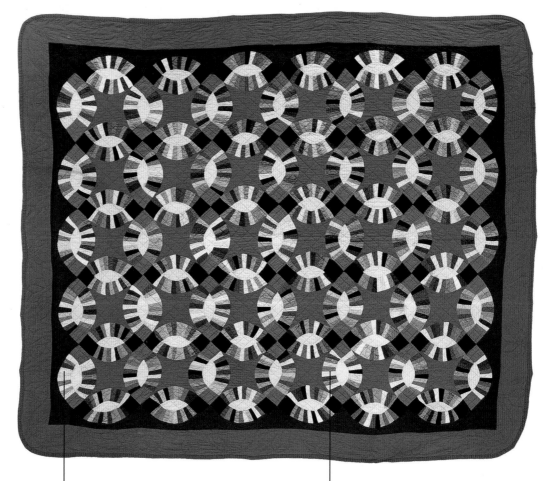

The rings are not perfectly round; the shape varies from pattern to pattern.

The solid crosshatching covering the entire surface of the rings is not typical of the double wedding ring design.

Amish Marriage

*W*EDDINGS ARE IMPORTANT *events in the community because they signify the perpetuation of the Amish way of life. The responsibility of raising a family is central to marriage and far more important than any notion of romance.*

Dating usually begins at the age of sixteen for a boy and between fourteen and sixteen for a girl. The youths attend Sunday evening singing sessions, held in the same house as the morning service, and use the opportunity to socialize and express interest in each other.

Many weddings can occur within one extended family because the community is so closely related.

Courting is conducted as secretly as possible. A boy may take a girl home after the Sunday service and see her every other Saturday evening, and events such as barn-raisings and weddings provide other opportunities to meet. Partners can be chosen from other Amish communities, although there is little contact between communities generally; first-cousin marriages are banned.

The prenuptial procedure starts when the boyfriend asks for a letter guaranteeing his good standing as a member of his church group. The letter is taken to the deacon of his girlfriend's group. The deacon then visits her house, acting as a "go-between," to tell her the boy would like to marry. By this point she is

well-prepared to accept. The procedure ensures that the girl cannot be forced into marriage by her parents or her boyfriend. A wedding date is decided and the intention to marry, along with the date of the event, is announced to the congregation at the Sunday service. The number of people invited depends on the size of the house where the wedding will be held. Often the invitation simply takes the form of "everyone over the age of twelve," or "everyone over the age of eighteen," or simply "everyone." Sometimes there may be as many as 400 guests.

The majority of weddings in Lancaster County take place in November, when the harvest is gathered but the really severe winter weather has not yet set in. Tuesdays and Thursdays are chosen to give the families time between Sunday services to prepare.

In Lancaster County, there is a good chance that an Amish woman will not actually change her surname while taking her husband's. Most Amish have one of six surnames: Beiler, Fisher, King, Miller, Lapp, or Stoltzfus.

The task of organizing the ceremony is divided between the friends and relatives of the bride's family. Before the ceremony itself, the bridal couple meet upstairs in the house with the bishop and elders who warn and advise them about married life. They then go downstairs for the ceremony. The bride and groom each have two attendants, and the bridal party welcomes the guests to the bride's home. The bride wears a new dress in a color of her choice, but not white, and she wears her white apron and cape for the last time. After the wedding she will wear the married woman's black apron and cape. The groom wears a black suit, a black waistcoat, a white shirt, a black bow-tie, and a black hat. There are no flowers, fancy clothes, or decorations. The ceremony varies according to region but always includes hymns, a sermon, and the words of marriage. In Lancaster County, these words are taken from the Gemein Ordnung, *the Amish book of service. Neither bride nor groom wears a ring.*

After the ceremony the rest of the day is spent eating, visiting, and, for the teenagers, special singing. The logistics of feeding such large numbers of people require detailed planning and much hard work. There are possibly three sittings at each meal and two meals, afternoon and evening, as well as snacks available throughout the day. The food varies according to community and region, but a typical meal includes chicken, stuffing, mashed potatoes, gravy, creamed celery, coleslaw, apple sauce, bread, butter, fruit pies, donuts, fruit salad, and coffee. One similarity to an "English" wedding is a wedding cake, which is either homemade or supplied by a bakery.

There is a special corner set aside for the bridal party, and everyone else eats at long tables and benches, as they would after Sunday service. More tolerant families invite relatives who have been excommunicated, or "shunned." These people are seated at separate tables, a little removed from the others.

Couples usually meet at Sunday singing sessions.

The newlyweds do not honeymoon; their wedding night is spent at the bride's house. She remains at home for the winter with visits from her husband, who lives principally at his parents' home. Traditionally, the young couple, along with other newlyweds, will visit members of the congregation who came to the wedding and receive their wedding gifts. The gifts are useful household items like furniture, bedding, kitchen utensils, gardening tools, and even canned food. The parents of the couple give more substantial gifts, perhaps even a house, land, or livestock.

In the spring, when all the furniture and household goods have been gathered, the young couple will move into their new home.

The responsibility of raising a family is central to marriage.

Making the Quilt

$\mathcal{T}$HE DOUBLE WEDDING RING PATTERN is among the most difficult of all patchwork designs and is not recommended for beginners. It is however, a lovely pattern for those who like a challenge and it works well using very small scraps in a random arrangement. To make a larger piece, simply increase the number of rings.

CUTTING GUIDE

Piece	Quantity	Size
A	24 yellow, gold, light green, green	Template page 118
B	24 dark green, red	Template page 118
C	12 gold, red	Template page 118
D	12 muslin (calico)	Template page 118
E	4 muslin (calico)	Template page 118

See page 126 for the total amount of fabric required to complete this quilt.

CUTTING

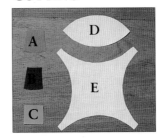

1 Trace the templates on page 118 and transfer to card or template plastic. Following the list of pieces required *(left)*, cut the A pieces first.

2 Cut two strips of fabric, double over to make four layers. Align one straight edge with the grain of the fabric and mark shape A. *Inset*: Using fabric scissors, cut out the shapes following the marked lines.

3 Following the method in Step 1, cut out shapes D and E from the background fabric.

4 For machine piecing you need to mark all the dots and center marks on each piece B, D, and E. For hand stitching you must also mark all seam allowances on the wrong side of each piece.

STITCHING

5 Chain-piece *(see page 115)* the A shapes in pairs of two colors, taking a ¼-inch (6-mm) seam along the straight edges.

6 Next piece the arcs by joining the two pairs of colors. *Inset*: In this design, half of the arcs are mirror images.

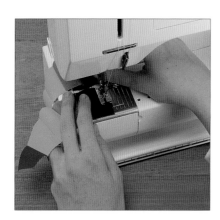

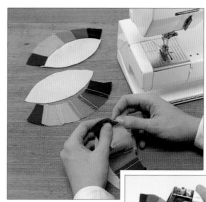

6 Add one B shape of each color at each end of the pieced arc. Follow the finished design *(below)* for color placement. Press the seams carefully to avoid stretching the curved edges. Check the shape of the arc against the template on page 118.

7 Pin and stitch one arc to each side of each shape D. Match the center seam of the arc with the center of shape D. *Inset:* Press the seams toward the outside edges.

8 Add the end squares (shape C). Mark the 1/4-inch (6-mm) seam allowances in one corner on the wrong side. Align the marked point at the end of shape D. Pin and stitch from the marked point to the outside edge of the arc. Repeat from the point to the other edge.

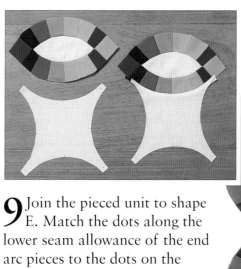

9 Join the pieced unit to shape E. Match the dots along the lower seam allowance of the end arc pieces to the dots on the "arms" of shape E. Match the center seams of the arcs to the central dots on shapes E. Stitch the curved seams first, working toward the outside of the piece being stitched in each case about 2–3 inches (5–7.5 cm) from the corner of the center section. Join the pieces following the numbers on the guide. Press all the seams to one side, working on the wrong side of the piece.

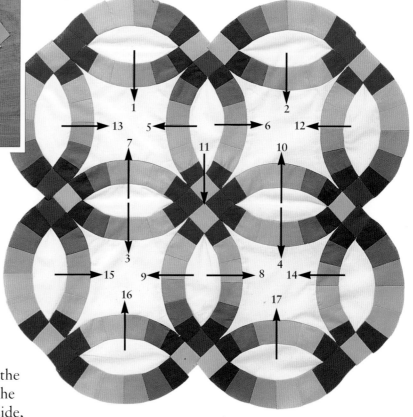

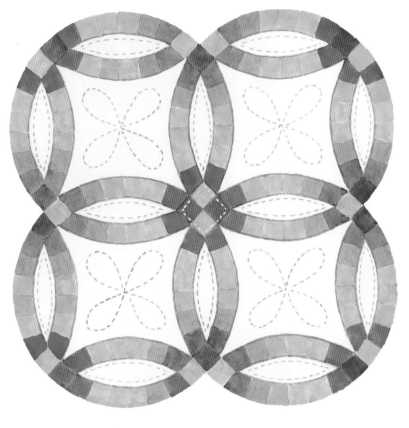

QUILTING

10 Add the backing and batting (wadding) *(see page 116)*, then quilt with matching thread using outline quilting within shape D and around the central diamond shape. Quilt a simple motif in the center of shape E *(see page 122)*.

BINDING

11 When the quilting is complete, trim away the edges of the batting and backing.

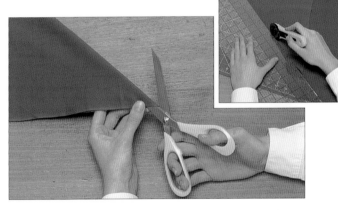

12 To bind the curved edges of the quilt, you need to cut the binding fabric on the bias. *Inset*: Cut bias strips measuring 2 inches (5 cm) wide.

13 Stitch the bias binding to the quilt top on the right side, taking a 1/4-inch (6-mm) seam and easing it gently around the curves as you work.

14 Turn the binding to the back and turn the raw edge under. Pin the binding in place and slipstitch by hand.

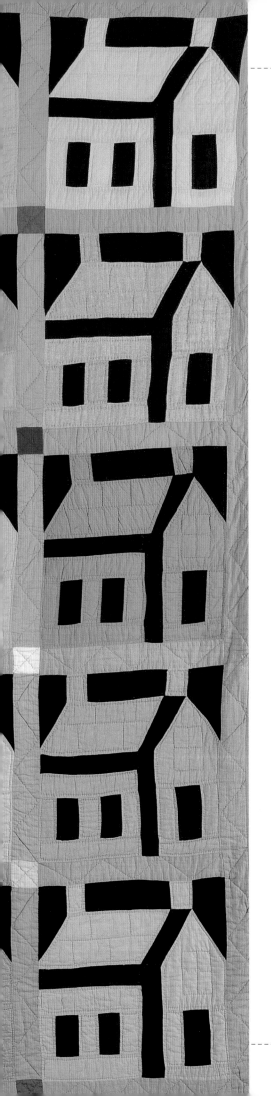

School-house

❖❖❖❖❖❖❖❖❖❖❖❖❖❖

*L*IKE MOST TRADITIONAL Amish patchwork, the Schoolhouse quilt is relatively simple and based on geometric shapes. The most notable difference between this design and other traditional patterns is that the work is representational. The abstraction of early Amish quilts is abandoned here and an actual object pictured. The schoolhouse itself has been reduced to its simplest form, although it retains its general characteristics and is immediately recognizable. The type of schoolhouse shown is the typical small, rural, one-room building of the nineteenth century, which is still in use among the twentieth-century Amish.

THE HISTORY OF THE PATTERN

The Schoolhouse pattern was developed and used by American patchworkers in the late nineteenth century. Early schoolhouses were often painted red, and enthusiastic use was made of the turkey red fabric that was fashionable in the second half of the nineteenth century, to create the quilts. The pattern may have been adopted by the Midwestern Amish first, because

Schoolhouse, *c.* 1920
This unusual Schoolhouse quilt has unexpected depths created by the subtle colors set off by splashes of pink and yellow.

it more closely resembles their patchwork – more block work and less intricate quilting – than the work of the Pennsylvania Amish. There are rarely any intricate quilting patterns on this quilt; most of the quilting follows the outline of the pieced blocks.

The Schoolhouse design was used among the Amish possibly as long as eighty or ninety years ago and may well have become a symbol of the battle for the Amish to keep their schools separate from the state-run educational system.

REPRESENTATIONAL IMAGES

The use of block work meant that there were smaller areas of interest in the quilt, rather than a large overall effect, and this allowed the formation of pictorial images. Patchwork designs featuring objects such as stars, baskets, stylized flowers, and wreaths, began to appear in the nineteenth century, even among the Amish.

As time went on and quiltmaking became a profitable industry for the Amish, they incorporated more and more "English" devices

Each house block is quilted with an unconventional feathered circle.

The sashing is crosshatched, while the border quilting consists of simple diagonal lines that run in a different direction on each side.

Schoolhouse, *c.* 1920
Nine-patch blocks have been used very cleverly in this quilt. They act as conventional corners in the sashing, but when placed in the outer sashing, they give the effect of overlapping into the border. The piecing, as on many old Schoolhouse quilts, is not perfect, but the irregularities lend charm to the piece. The colors are traditional, exemplifying the fabrics of the early twentieth century. The dark fabric of the border and sashing not only frame but also emphasize each individual schoolhouse.

into their quilts. The use of white fabrics also became more common, in contrast to the dark and subdued quilts of the nineteenth century. Modern quilt buyers demand lighter, more delicate quilts. Following the invention of easy-care fabrics, such as polyester, the Amish can use these paler shades more readily. White was rarely used in the past due to its impracticality.

The Amish quiltmakers also introduced printed fabrics and pastel colors, and took greater liberties with the patterns they used. Even sampler-type block quilts appear, where each block illustrates a different image. However, the Amish only incorporated these features in quilts they intended to sell, and plain, traditional quilts were still made for the home.

The Schoolhouse pattern depicts an image that is central to Amish life, so in some ways the quilt is typical of Amish quilting traditions, despite its pictorial imagery.

Schoolhouse, 1910-20

The positioning of each separate schoolhouse block on this quilt is typical of older patchworks. Very often, blocks were placed facing outward from the middle, echoing the center medallion effect. There is more of interest on this quilt than first meets the eye. The four-patch corner blocks, the small triangles in the outer sashing on the sides, and the bright orange binding all lift an otherwise ordinary quilt to greater heights.

The dark sashing, echoed in the outer border, creates a strong secondary pattern.

The four-patch corner squares are placed with the colors at random.

Education

THE AMISH maintain their own schools independent of the state-run school system. Until early in the twentieth century, Amish children went to school with their "English" neighbors because all schools were small and local. In the 1950s the state created enormous, rural consolidated schools that required bussing Amish children all over the county. The Amish felt it necessary to keep their children separate in order to maintain their traditions. There were numerous clashes with state authorities, particularly in Pennsylvania, and some Amish fathers were imprisoned for refusing to send their children to state schools.

In the Lancaster County disputes, the first compromise was made when an interpretation of the vocational school rules allowed an Amish teacher to teach children over fourteen years of age at home for three hours a week. The situation was finally resolved in 1972 when the Supreme Court ruled that the Amish have the right to maintain separate schools.

Amish schoolhouses are small, one-room buildings, often without indoor plumbing, electricity, or central heating. They have changed little over the past century, and are still recognizable from the Little Red School-house quilts. The schools are old-fashioned in structure, furnishing, and education, and have

Amish schools provide a strong cohesive force for maintaining family, religion, and society.

about twenty-five pupils from the ages of six to fourteen. The children are well disciplined, and are expected to sit up straight and pay attention at all times. They learn such subjects as reading, arithmetic, history, geography, English, and German by rote and recitation. The school may be the first opportunity a child has to speak English.

The curriculum is not broad; there are no art or drama classes, computer studies, or science laboratories. Music is not specifically taught, but unaccompanied singing does take place. There are songbooks specifically for schools, and some children learn to play the recorder. There are no specific religious studies; religion is included as part of the coursework in other subjects. Facts are carefully learned, but creative thought and enquiring questions are not encouraged. Despite the differences with mainstream schools, studies show that Amish children equal or surpass "English" children in factual examinations given at the age of eleven or twelve.

Amish children start school at the age of six.

Reading is one of the Amish people's greatest pleasures, and school libraries are filled with books chosen by parents and teachers. The Amish also love sports, especially baseball, and children play enthusiastically without a sense of competition. Games take place in a friendly atmosphere and are played in groups, as singular sports are considered prideful.

On leaving school at the age of fourteen, boys begin to work seriously in their trade, becoming more involved with farm work or apprenticing with the blacksmith, harness maker, or carpenter. Girls go home to help their mothers with siblings and housework, learning the cooking, washing, gardening, and sewing skills that will be their work for the rest of their lives. Because of the vocational requirement from state education, Amish children go to school three hours a week between the ages of fourteen and fifteen. Some may go on to take correspondence courses, but they have no ambition for higher education qualifications or a professional life. The Amish's greatest goal is to marry, get a farm, and have a family.

In most cases school is an extension of home life. Parents are actively involved, building the schools, purchasing the books, hiring the teachers, and administrating. Teachers are usually young women chosen for their good Christian character who may teach for three or four years and then leave to get married.

A traditional red schoolhouse in Lancaster County.

The teachers have no particular training and no more than eight years of education, the same as their eldest pupils. Some may do a Graduate Equivalency Diploma or correspondence courses, but most "Plain" teachers teach by setting a good example in school, at home, and in church. They are constantly observed by their pupils.

The school system is old-fashioned and has changed little over the past 100 years. The curriculum is limited and buildings are quaint, but for the Amish the schools provide a strong cohesive force for maintaining family, religion, and society. The Amish feel a good basic education is essential to avoid becoming a burden on society, but their way of life demands little formal education, instead treasuring the school as an integral part of the growth and development of the Amish child.

School children are well disciplined and learn by rote and recitation.

Making the Quilt

*T*HIS BLOCK CAN BE PIECED BY hand or machine. For hand piecing mark 1/4-inch (6-mm) seam allowances on the wrong side of each piece. For machine piecing it is easier to match seams on pieces with sharp angles, if some of the allowances are marked as indicated in the steps. To make a bed quilt, increase the number of blocks but keep the size of the house blocks and the proportions of the sashing and borders the same.

CUTTING GUIDE

Piece	Quantity	Measurement
A	2 red	$1^1/2$ x $2^1/4$ in (4 x 5.5 cm)
D	2 red	$2^1/8$ x $3^1/2$ in (5 x 9 cm)
E	1 red	$1^1/2$ x $4^1/2$ in (4 x 11.5 cm)
F	2 red	$1^1/2$ x $5^1/2$ in (4 x 14 cm)
G	2 red	$1^1/2$ x $3^1/2$ in (4 x 9 cm)
H	2 red	$1^3/8$ x $3/4$ in (3.5 x 2 cm)
J	1 red	2 x $3^1/2$ in (5 x 9 cm)
Cut B and C using the templates on page 119		
II	1 cream	$4^1/4$ x $2^1/4$ in (11 x 5.5 cm)
VII	1 cream	$1^3/8$ x $3^1/2$ in (3.5 x 9 cm)
VIII	4 cream	$1^3/8$ x $1^7/8$ in (3.5 x 5 cm)
Cut I, III, IV, V and VI using the templates on page 119		

See page 126 for the total amount of fabric required.

CUTTING

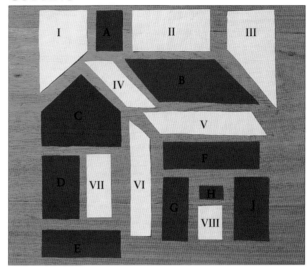

1 To make one schoolhouse block, cut out the pieces following the instructions given in the Cutting Guide *(left)*.

STITCHING

2 Join pieces in sections, starting with the windows. Join one piece VIII to each side of a piece H, taking $1/4$-inch (6-mm) seams.

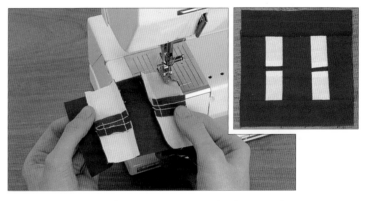

3 Join the window sections to the long side of each piece J, and add one piece G to each side. *Inset:* Add a piece F to the top and bottom edges to finish the "wall" block.

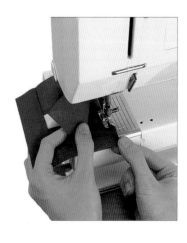

4 Make the front door section by applying one piece D to each side of piece VII. Then add pieces C and E, following the diagram carefully.

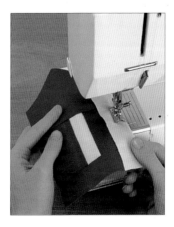

5 Press the seams and then add the long piece VI to the inside long edge of the front door section.

6 Apply strip IV to the end of piece B and add strip V along the bottom edge. Match the beginning and end of each $^{1}/_{4}$-inch (6-mm) seam. *Inset:* The basic elements are now complete. Join the window section to the door section.

7 To add the roof, mark the seam allowances and start stitching from the apex. Stop $^{1}/_{4}$ inch (6 mm) from the bottom edge of the roof piece. Raise the presser foot and turn the piece to join the bottom edge to the window section.

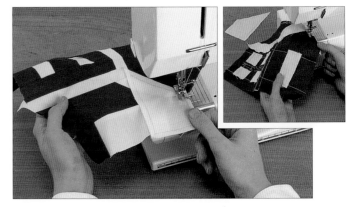

8 Apply one chimney A to each end of piece II, then sew this piece to the roof. Again, mark the seam allowance on the oblique seams. Start by matching the apex of the roof to the allowance on the chimney piece.

9 Add pieces I and III to the top corners to complete the block. *Inset:* Match the seam allowances at the inner point on each piece and stitch outward, first toward the top of the block, then out to the side, turning the needle.

10 The single block, measuring 9 inches (23 cm) square, is now complete. For this wall-hanging you need four schoolhouse blocks.

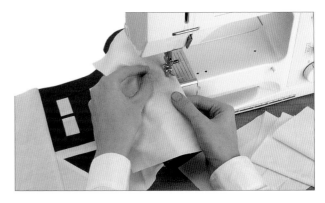

11 Apply $4^{1}/_{2}$-inch (11.5-cm) sashing strips to the left side of each block and join the blocks in pairs. Add a strip to the right edge.

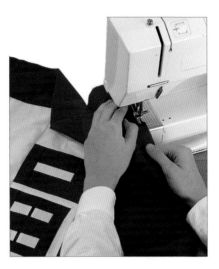

12 Join the paired units with a long strip of sashing, then add sashing to the top and bottom edges.

13 Finally, add 5-inch (13-cm) wide red border strips to the sides and then to the top and bottom edges.

14 The quilt top is now complete and ready for quilting. Add the backing and batting (wadding) *(see page 116)* before you start to quilt.

QUILTING

15 The main elements of the house are outline-quilted in black, 1/4 inch (6 mm) from the seam. The background is quilted using an evenly spaced diagonal line, from bottom left to top right.

16 Mark each diagonal line 1 inch (2.5 cm) apart with a strip of 1/4-inch (6-mm) masking tape, then stitch that line before marking and quilting the next.

17 The quilt is backed and bound in red using the back-to-front method *(see page 93).*

Baskets

❖❖❖❖❖❖❖❖❖❖❖❖❖❖❖❖❖❖

*T*HE BASKETS PATTERN is an example of the block-style patchwork sewn by Midwestern Amish quiltmakers in the late nineteenth century. Midwestern Amish settlers were more recent arrivals to the United States and to patchwork and quilting techniques. They did not adopt the quilting traditions already established in the east, such as the Center Diamond and Bars patterns, but picked up early American block patchwork.

The Midwestern communities were farther apart than those in the east, and as communications were primitive, these satellite groups made their own rules and regulations, within limits, and relied more on their non-Amish neighbors than on the directions of the conservative ministers in the east. Consequently, more worldly influences crept into their quiltmaking. Although plain Amish colors were used, in many areas elaborate patchwork patterns were permitted, and as a result their quilts have a vibrant quality.

The first block piecing accomplished by the Amish was the Nine-Patch and its variations, then more elaborate patterns were introduced, such as the Baskets, and eventually the Starflower (see page 95), which are more representational than traditional quilts.

Fruit Basket, *c.* 1935
The magnificent quilting – chrysanthemums encircled by sunbursts, twining violets, and bows – combined with spectacular color mean that this quilt was a "best" quilt.

MIDWESTERN FEATURES

Whereas the traditional Lancaster County Amish quilts are distinguished by corner blocks and very wide – 12–15 inch (30–38 cm) – borders, the Amish quilts made in Ohio, Indiana, Iowa, and other Midwestern states have narrow borders or sometimes no border at all. The East Coast quilts also typically feature one main design and large expanses of colored fabric, allowing for elaborate quilting effects, but the Midwestern versions are made using much smaller pieces of fabric.

Other important differences between the two groups relate to the type of fabric used and to the choice of color. Whereas wool is traditional in Pennsylvania, cotton is seen predominantly in Midwestern quilts, although sateen, twill, and flannel were also often used. The warmer colors of yellow, orange, and red appear in Midwestern quilts, and sometimes white is used, but these colors rarely appear in early Lancaster County quilts. Part of the reason for the different uses of color lies in the geographic situation of the Midwest Amish. Fabric was

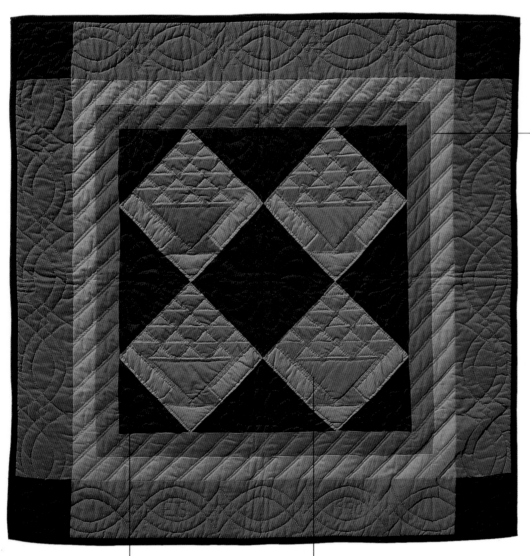

The double diagonal line is a good alternative to crosshatching for quilting backgrounds and borders.

Basket, c. 1990
The unusual color combination in this quilt demonstrates the uninhibited creativity of Amish quilters. This Basket pattern is beautifully constructed, with the colors of the baskets repeated in the three borders. This version of the Basket block contains smaller pieces than Amish women normally used, but the popularity of the design introduced them to the intricate work being done by more worldly women, and must have appealed to them as a frugal way to use even the smallest of scraps.

The central flower motif has been halved to fill the outer triangles and quartered for the corner triangles.

Outline quilting is used around each section of background fabric in the main blocks.

more scarce, and women had to use what was available since shops were almost unknown and settlements far apart. Although the Amish woman would use only conventional Amish colors such as blacks, blues, and greens for clothing, printed fabrics were sometimes used in quilts, but only for the quilt backing.

THE ORIGIN OF THE BASKETS PATTERN

The pieced Baskets pattern dates from the 1850s and was developed from the appliquéd baskets that appeared on album quilts. By the early twentieth century, the East Coast Amish were making Baskets quilts, too.

Many different versions of this design exist, such as the Grape Basket, Cherry Basket, Fruit Basket, Flower Basket, Basket of Scraps, Flower Pot, and even Cake Stand. The Basket of Scraps, which includes a pieced basket and colorful diamond-shaped patches for the flowers, is one of the simplest. The Cherry Basket is made up in two contrasting fabrics, cut in triangles. The Fruit Basket pattern appears frequently among Pennsylvania

Flowerpot, c. 1990
This simple, as yet unquilted, top for a Basket wall hanging, finds its beauty in the colors used, and the starkness of the dark blue inner border and corner squares against the white background and outer border is striking. As in so many of the more intricate patchwork patterns, the quilting will play a fairly minor role. When patchwork pieces are so small and numerous, simple quilting motifs are required, with bursts of creative stitching on the borders.

The use of the three primary colors, set against a white background, is unusual in Amish quiltmaking.

The dark blue triangles set toward the apex of the diamond shapes alters the visual balance of the Basket blocks.

Amish, probably because it lends itself so well to the use of just two plain colors. In black and blue, or red and green, it is stunning; in delicate printed shades, it is pretty. The Flower Basket is made by Amish and non-Amish alike and could be constructed in any number of colors, but is striking in plains. The baskets themselves were, early on, made in brown, white, or yellow by non-Amish quilters and were often considered interesting enough to stand on their own. Handles sometimes appear on the baskets, and if so, they are usually appliquéd on after the piecing is done. Some quilters appliqué colorful flowers in the basket and others quilt flowers on top. The pattern requires strongly contrasting fabrics to enliven the design and can be beautifully accomplished using the range of solid, jewel-like Amish colors.

Baskets, *c.* 1990
The dramatic colors of this wall-hanging, made by the same quilter as the piece shown on page 86 and quilted in an identical pattern, are very typical of the Lancaster County Amish tradition. Although Amish women are allowed to choose from a wide range of plain solid colors for their dresses, blue is the hue most often worn. The combination of the two blues and black in this quilt perfectly represents Amish women, their clothes, and their quilts.

The corner motif is a simplified version of the central flower motif.

Migration

ETWEEN 1720 and 1780, the first small groups of Amish emigrated to Pennsylvania. The guaranteed religious freedom and the extremely fertile farmland convinced the Amish that emigration was the answer to the years of persecution and famine that they had suffered since founding their community in Germany, in the late seventeenth century.

A second wave of immigration into America, encouraged by economic hardship and war in Europe, started around 1815 and continued until 1860. This second group traveled to the Midwest in Ohio, Illinois, Indiana, Iowa, and Ontario. Some settled first in Pennsylvania, then moved on.

The Amish moved around North America for a number of reasons including marriage, climate, and most importantly, farmland. These new immigrants were viewed by the conservative Amish as a corrupting influence because their lifestyle was too often patterned on that of their non-Amish neighbors. Interestingly, this was reflected in their quilts, with the work of Midwestern Amish far more worldly, colorful, and exuberant than the muted work of the Lancaster County Amish.

Migration slowed dramatically around the turn of the century. Few Amish were arriving from Europe, and those already

Church meetings bring the community together.

settled were establishing homes and communities. Settled communities became the norm, and most Amish families became strongly opposed to moving. The first twentieth-century migration from Lancaster County occurred in the 1940s, as a result of a school dispute.

Modern migration occurs slowly and often without enthusiasm. The Amish are hesitant to move, many valuing the closeness of the family over the necessity to farm. But by the 1970s it became harder to buy farmland. An increase in tourism brought greater temptation for the Amish to move into the outside world. These pressures have renewed Amish thoughts of moving to find farmland and peace and quiet.

> **The Amish migrate in order to find affordable farmland and preserve the Amish way of life.**

Making the Quilt

ASKETS, OF COURSE, COME IN various shapes and sizes. This version is straightforward to make as a double four-patch block — the complicated part is working with the right-angle triangles. Fifteen blocks could be combined to make a single bed quilt. This quilt is bound using the back to front method.

CUTTING GUIDE

Piece	Quantity	Size
Basket block	2 rust, 1 of each contrasting color, 1 black	4³/4 in (12 cm) square
	5 rust	4³/8 in (11 cm) square
	1 rust, 1 black	8¹/2 in (21.5 cm) square
Corner triangles	2 black	11¹/2 in (29 cm) square
Border strips	4 rust	4in (10 cm) wide
Border squares	4 black	4 in (10 cm) square

See page 126 for the total amount of fabric required.

CUTTING

1 Following the instructions given in the Cutting Guide *(left)*, cut out the pieces required *(see inset)*. You can cut the 4³/8-inch (11-cm) squares from a strip of fabric, measuring carefully.

2 For the basket, cut each 4³/4-inch (12-cm) square in half across the diagonal to make 14 right-angle triangles.

3 Cut the large 8¹/2-inch (21.5-cm) squares. Use a square ruler to make sure that all the edges are equal.

STITCHING

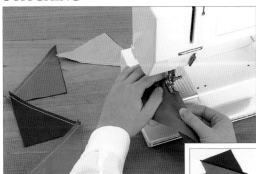

4 Chain-piece the smaller triangles together into squares *(see page 115)*. Join one of each contrasting color to rust; one light blue to black; one purple to black, one dark blue to green. *Inset:* Press all seams to the darker side.

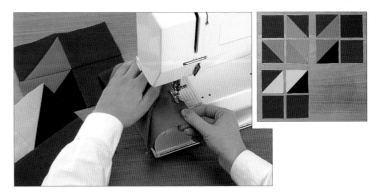

5 Lay out the pieced squares together with the 4³/8-inch (11-cm) rust squares before you combine the pieces *(see inset)*. Join the pairs first, then join the paired strips to make three four-patch units.

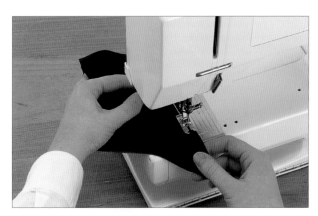

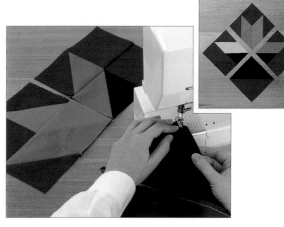

6 Next, join the large black and rust triangles to make the fourth unit of the block – the bottom of the basket.

7 Join the pieced squares in pairs with a ¼-inch (6-mm) seam, following the layout *(see inset)*. Join the pairs into the finished block.

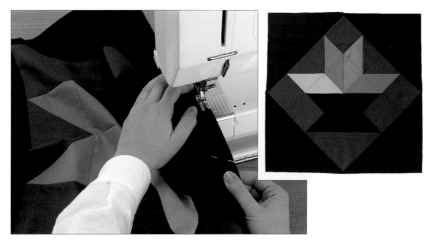

8 Join the large black triangles to the sides of the basket block. Pin the center of the long side of each triangle to the center of one side of the block. Stitch two opposite sides first, then add the two remaining sides. The block is now complete *(see inset)*.

9 Next, add the borders. Make the border strips by chain-piecing one black corner square to the end of each border strip.

10 With right sides together, apply the first border strip to the basket block. The corner square should overhang the top edge. Start stitching 4–5 inches (10–13 cm) below the corner of the block. Mark the points where the triangles meet in the center of each side of the block with a pin, and avoid stitching over them.

11 Add the remaining strips. When the fourth strip has been stitched in place, return to the overhanging corner square and finish stitching the seam.

12 Press all the seams to one side on the wrong side of the quilt. The finished block is now ready to be marked with the quilting patterns.

MARKING

13 Using dressmaker's chalk and a ruler, mark the crosshatching across the basket.

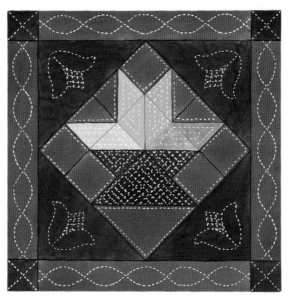

14 Mark the quilting motifs for the tulips and outer border *(see page 124)* following the diagram and add batting (wadding) and backing *(see page 116)*. Work the quilting.

BACK TO FRONT BINDING

15 When the quilting is complete, trim away the batting. *Inset:* Then trim the backing to leave a 2-inch (5-cm) border.

16 With dressmaker's chalk, mark a 45-degree angle plus a 1/2-inch (1.3-cm) allowance and trim.

17 Turn the edge over so the raw edge of the backing meets the raw edge of the top. Fold again over the top of the quilt and pin in place. Slipstitch all round.

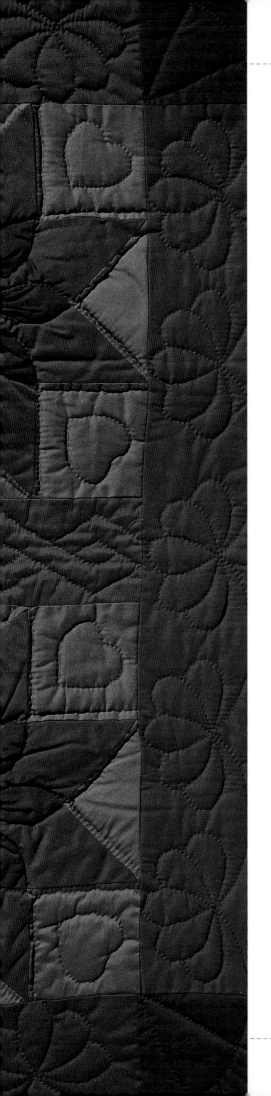

Star-flower

❖❖❖❖❖❖❖❖❖❖❖❖❖

HE STARFLOWER, also called the Dahlia, is a beautiful block-style design developed about twenty years ago as a variation on the nineteenth-century Eight Point, or Le Moyne, Star. Especially popular in the Midwest and among more liberal Amish communities, the pattern is bold, yet pretty. Although spectacular when completed in true Amish colors, the design is most frequently made in printed patterned fabrics to appeal to "English" buyers.

Each block is pieced as an eight-point star, with the gathered petals of the inner flower pieced into the star and the flower center appliquéd on top. Many different compositions are possible, with the blocks divided by sashing, alternating with plain blocks, or set on point as diamonds. The stars can also be made so that their points touch when the blocks are joined.

BLOCK PATCHWORK BEGINNINGS

The nineteenth century saw the proliferation of the block style in America. When a few scraps of fabric

Starflower, c. 1990
Because the Starflower, or Dahlia, is most frequently seen in pretty printed floral fabrics, the depth and drama of this version worked in typical Amish colors are surprising.

Home and Household

THE DAY-TO-DAY LIFE of an Amish woman may seem old-fashioned and unnecessarily arduous to outsiders, but can be highly satisfying. Because the women have large families with an average of seven children, and mothering is considered to be of utmost importance, most of their work is home- and family-oriented.

All household chores take time. Although the women have a lot of work to do, they have help and support readily available. Their mothers, sisters, aunts, and cousins all live nearby and are ready to lend a hand. It is not unusual for four or five Amish women to get together to spring clean one house, then the next week clean another. Much work, such as quilting, barn-raising, harvesting, and cleaning, is done in groups.

The Amish have no dietary restrictions, and plain, fresh, wholesome food is served from a solid fuel or natural gas stove.

Cooking is time-consuming without modern electrical appliances. Despite the hardships, the women enjoy entertaining, and Amish households are usually alive with family and friends.

Sewing also takes a great amount of an Amish woman's time. Traditionally, she

Amish households are usually alive with family and friends.

makes the dresses, aprons, capes, shirts, trousers, and jackets for her children, her husband, and herself. She also makes quilts, a necessity in a house without central heating. She quilts by herself, or with her mother and her sisters, or at a Quilting Bee. The Bee is a typical Amish social occasion with talk, food, and work intermingled throughout the day. Women of all abilities may be asked to a Quilting Bee; some prepare food, some look after the children, and nearly all take their turn at the quilting frame.

An increasing number of Amish women run their own businesses from home, most are quilt-related. Running such a business, however, takes time and effort, and this has sometimes forced changes. Occasionally, prepared food and ready-made clothes are purchased from other Amish women. Although the Amish woman's work has broadened considerably, it remains firmly within the confines of the family and home.

A Quilting Bee is an opportunity to socialize.

had been saved, early settlers would sew them together into a small designed square or block, which would later be joined with other blocks to create quilts. This process saved fabric, space, and time, and there was no need to handle large pieces of fabric when piecing.

Block patchwork also allowed for flexibility of purpose. One block will usually be big enough for a pillow cover; four blocks can be made into a wall-hanging; eight to twelve blocks into a throw; and as many as fifty-six blocks make a full-size quilt.

There are two basic categories of block style quilts; those in which the blocks stand alone, such as Starflower, Ohio Star, and Baskets (see page 85) and those in which blocks have been joined together as parts of the overall design, such as Log Cabin and Drunkards Path.

Block patchwork requires controlled quilting with little creativity. Stitches are placed on the seam, called the "ditch," of the patchwork, or more effectively just off the seam. The quilting accentuates the intricate patchworking, rather than acting as a separate decorative element.

Starflower, *c.* 1990
Amish quilters today make decorative, delicately colored quilts for sale. This is an exquisite example of a modern Amish block set off with elaborate quilting and gracefully scalloped borders. The quality of the piecing, and of the quilting that provides the quilt's fabulous texture, is outstanding. Amish quilts made for sale are sewn by only one or two women, unlike those made for their own use, which are often put together and quilted by many hands at quilting bees.

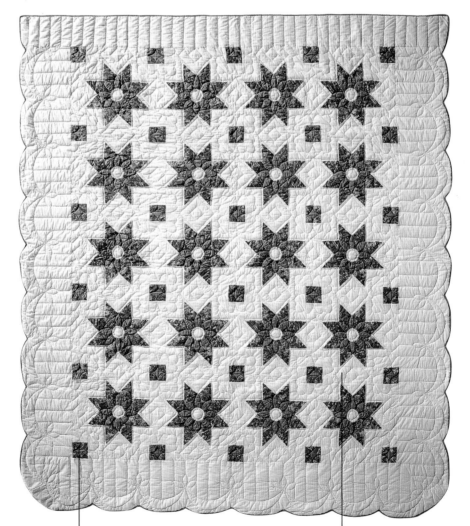

The corner blocks in the sashing, as well as the scalloped border and the floral fabric, are worldly elements on this quilt made to sell.

The quilting motifs draw together the background and the sashing to make a beautifully textured secondary pattern.

Making the Quilt

*T*HIS SLIGHTLY TRICKY PATTERN, an embellished eight-point star, is not recommended for the novice; but for more experienced quilters, it repays the effort necessary to assemble it, and the quilting is simple and straightforward. A bed quilt can be assembled using more blocks separated by single sashing strips.

CUTTING GUIDE

Piece	Quantity	Measurement
Petal shape A	8 red	template page 120
Star shape B	8 blue	template page 120
Circle shape C	1 blue	template page 120
Squares	4 green	4½ in (11.5 cm) square
	2 green	5 in (13 cm) square cut into diagonals
Inner border strips	3 purple	2½ in (6 cm) wide
	3 green	2½ in (6 cm) wide
Outer border strips	4 blue	3¾ in (9.5 cm) wide
Border squares	4 red	3¾ in (9.5 cm) square

See page 126 for the total amount of fabric required to complete this quilt.

CUTTING

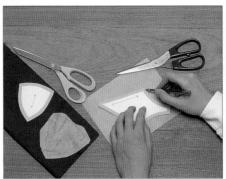

1 Trace the templates for shapes A, B, and C onto card or template plastic. Make paper patterns and pin to the material to cut out. *Inset*: Cut out all the elements following the Cutting Guide. Cut the 5-inch (13-cm) squares in half along the diagonal to make triangles.

STITCHING

2 Set the sewing machine on the longest stitch length and sew a gathering thread at the top of each shape A, leaving long threads at the beginning and end.

3 Pin and stitch one shape A to the right-hand curved edge of a shape B. Attach the point of shape A to the bottom end of the curve. Repeat to make eight identical units. *Inset*: Press the seams toward the blue side.

4 To four of the units, add a green triangle along the right-hand straight edge of shape B. Be careful not to catch the seam allowance into the stitching.

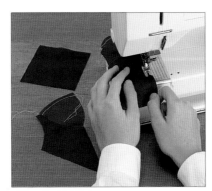

5 To the remaining four units, add a green square along the right-hand straight edge of shape B.

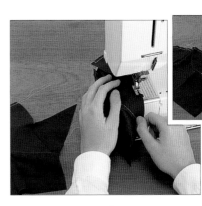

6 Join a triangle unit to a square unit. Stitch the straight edges first, then pin and stitch the curved seam *(see inset)*. Repeat to make four units and press.

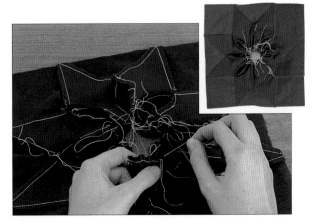

7 Join the pieced units from Step 6 in pairs, then join the pairs into a square. As in Step 6, stitch the straight seams first, then the curved edges. *Inset*: Press the seams flat.

8 Lay the square flat and carefully pull up the gathering threads until the center lies flat *(see inset)*.

9 Cut a circle from paper using the inner ring on the template for shape C on page 120. Pin and baste (tack) the blue fabric circle to the paper template.

10 Pin the circle over the central hole, positioning the pins between the red petals. Adjust the gathering. Baste the circle in place and slipstitch in place. Remove the basting threads and paper circle.

11 Apply the purple inner border to the finished block, sewing the top and bottom strips first, then adding the side strips. Repeat for the green middle border.

12 Assemble the outer border strips by chain-piecing *(see page 115)* a red corner square to each blue strip.

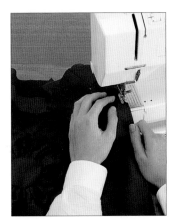

13 Apply the first outer strip by placing the top of the strip at the corner of the square with the outer corner overhanging. Begin stitching 6 inches (15 cm) down from the top edge.

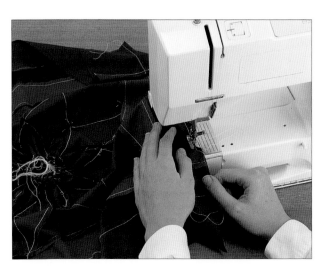

14 Add the remaining strips, matching the corner seams precisely. Finish stitching the first strip by sewing up to the top edge.

15 The quilt top is now complete and ready for quilting. Press the seams carefully on the reverse side.

MARKING

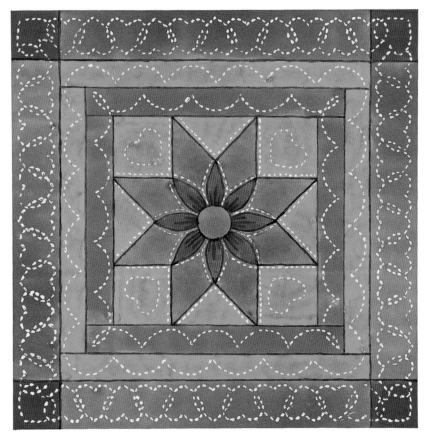

17 Trace the template on page 125 and mark the inner border pattern. Note that the template is equal to half of one side.

18 Add the batting and backing, and baste the layers together. Work all the quilting by hand, then remove the basting and bind the edges *(see page 117)*.

16 The diagram shows the placement of the quilting patterns. The hearts on the outer border alternate position and overlap. Use the template on page 123.

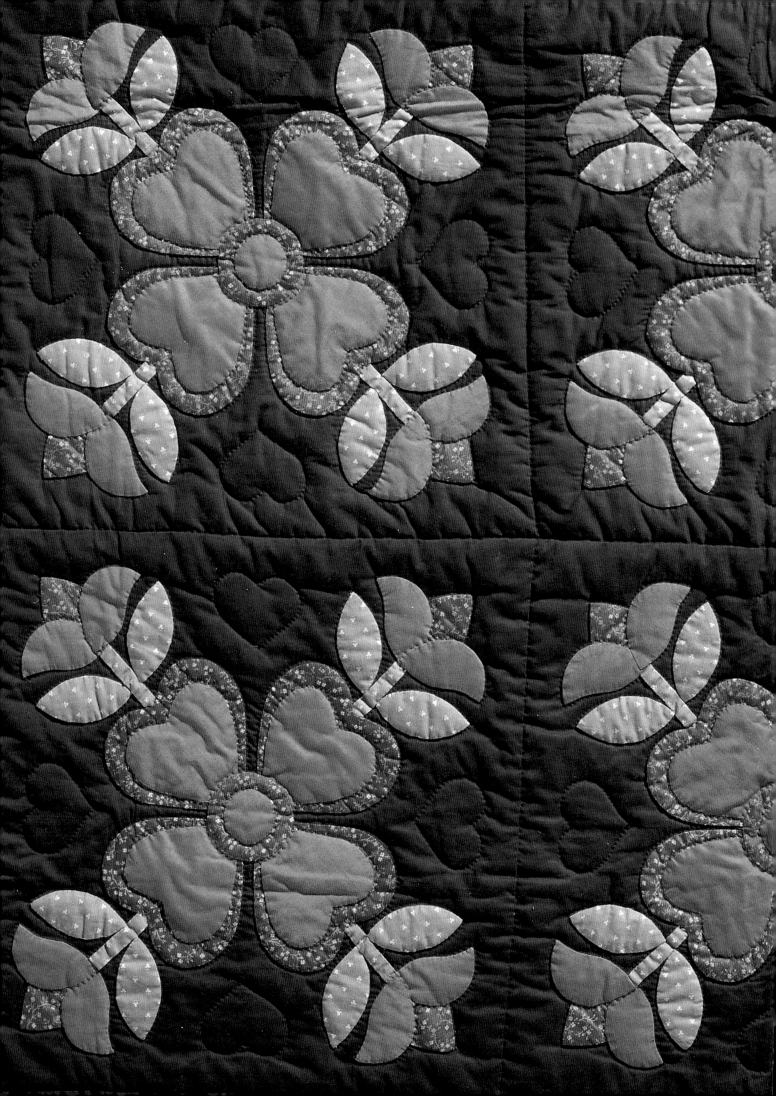

Lancaster Rose

❖❖❖-❖-❖❖-❖-❖❖-❖-❖❖-❖-❖❖-❖-❖❖-❖-❖❖-❖-❖❖❖

A MODERN QUILTING DESIGN based on appliqué techniques, the Lancaster Rose pattern was created in 1976 in the bicentennial year of American Independence, as a tribute to the quilt-makers' home of Lancaster, Pennsylvania.

In fifteenth-century England and during the Wars of the Roses, the Yorkists were represented by the white rose and the Lancastrians by the red rose; these traditions were taken up by the American towns of York and Lancaster, which lie approximately thirty miles apart on either side of the Susquehana River. A clever adaptation of the English red rose was chosen to represent Lancaster.

MOTIFS AND COLORS

The rose motif used in the Lancaster Rose quilt has many forerunners in quilting and needlework history. Similar rose appliqué patterns exist from the nineteenth and early twentieth centuries, such as the Rose of Sharon, Wild Rose, Wreath of Roses, and Whig

Lancaster Rose, *c*. 1990
The beautiful roses appliquéd onto a dusky blue background give charm and sophistication to this unconventional version of the Lancaster Rose pattern.

Rose. The rose motif may have also been influenced by the Pennsylvania Dutch, as stylized flowers are found in much of the painting and stencilwork of southern Germany.

Another feature of the Lancaster Rose quilt is that some of the piecework uses patterned fabric. The original color combination is red with green leaves on a white background – colors that also are a feature of the Baltimore album quilts of the nineteenth century. Red and green were strong dyes that could be relied on

to hold color for many years. Other shades and prints or solids may be used, and the quilt is now often seen in all colors, from blue and violet to pink and yellow.

APPLIQUÉ TRADITIONS

The pattern relies on appliqué, a method that was not traditionally Amish, nor American. Embroidered appliqué has existed in Europe since the thirteenth and fourteenth centuries, and during medieval times was used in flags,

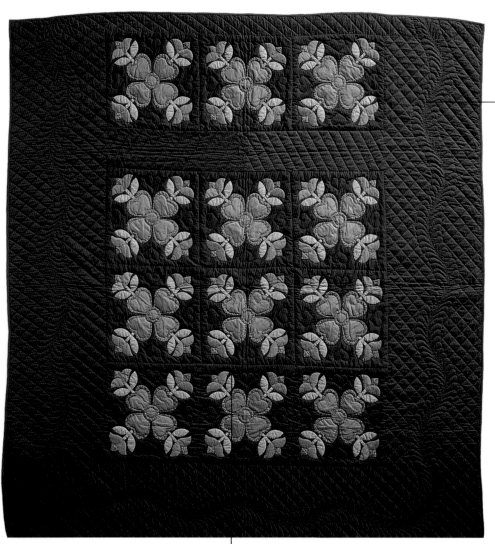

The close-spaced feathered cable is exquisitely stitched.

The judicious use of the mini-print fabrics that mark this as a sale quilt do not detract from an overall Amish "feel."

Lancaster Rose, *c.* 1990
Although the colors used in this Lancaster Rose quilt (detail on page 102) are dramatic, they are not traditional. The original Lancaster Roses were red with green leaves as dictated by the historical rose emblem of the aristocratic English family of Lancasters, from whom the county takes its name. This Amish quilt represents an interesting contrast between modern appliqué and a traditional blue border covered with quilting patterns that are among the oldest used by Amish women.

banners, and on military dress. While European quiltmakers had a long history of using the appliqué technique, their early American counterparts were block-style patchworkers. Settlers on farms did frugal patchwork, while ladies in the cities created appliquéd works of art. However, some farming wives did make appliqué quilts, but these were for "best."

Some of the most sought-after antique quilts in the United States are the magnificent Baltimore album appliqué quilts, made in the 1840s by the women of Baltimore to celebrate their lives and their city. These quilts featured floral and patriotic themes and were often signed by the quilter.

Amish women rarely made these bright, time-consuming, decorative quilts. However, they have become more enthusiastic about appliqué in recent years, and most of their innovative designs now entail some use of the technique. While non-Amish patchworkers are

Lancaster Rose, *c.* 1990
This appealing Lancaster Rose wall-hanging is an excellent example of the differences between modern and traditional work. Here the fabric is new not scrap, printed not plain; the appliqué pictorial not abstract; the effect planned not random. This is the sort of needlework found in large numbers in Amish quilt shops today, made to appeal to the general public.

The appliquéd hearts on the outer border have been repeated as quilting motifs in the white background triangles.

The Rose block is set on point within the background, giving the effect of a Center Diamond.

creating modern abstract quilts, the Amish are now moving from geometric abstracts to picture quilts, and their appliqué work embraces the beauty of nature and color in such motifs as birds, flowers, fruit, ribbons, and bows. Hearts have been used for more than 200 years.

THE APPLIQUÉ TECHNIQUE

Appliqué is the process of sewing one material to another by means of the hemming, appliqué stitch. The raw edges of the cut pieces are turned under and sewn in place neatly. Keeping all the appliquéd pieces flat and smooth is a time-consuming and tedious job. Curved patterns and shapes, particularly circles, flowers, and fruit, work best when appliquéd rather than pieced. Although the technique is a departure from the traditional quilting of the Amish, many fine examples of appliquéd quilts exist that evoke the spirit of the Amish.

The quilting is worked, unusually, in light-colored thread.

Lancaster Rose, c. 1990
This sophisticated Lancaster Rose quilt is made of fashionable modern fabrics in popular colors. The appliqué work, like all Amish appliqué, is beautifully hand sewn, and the piece is carefully arranged and carefully planned, with the rose-red binding an echo of the central circle and the dark blue used in each element of the quilt. Decorative rather than functional, this piece, in spite of its traditionally crosshatched background, lies at the opposite end of the spectrum from the orginal utilitarian scrap quilts made by the Amish such as Center Diamond or Bars.

The simple diagonal lines of stitching on the outer border are twice the width of the crosshatching.

Economics and Trade

*T*HE AMISH REMAIN *independent of the world, but modern society encroaches all the time. The economic realities of owning property and running businesses mean the Amish must find ways to work out compromises with the outside world without sacrificing their values.*

In the 1990s only about fifty percent of Amish men farm. Amish land holdings have expanded, but cannot keep up with the increase in the Amish population. As a result, the Amish have developed small businesses near the farms. Some are builders, carpenters, blacksmiths, wheelwrights, and animal sellers, while others run quilt and craft shops, bakeries, and produce markets. Their workmanship is characterized by great attention to detail and quality. The businesses are small – most have as few as six employees – but successful. The Amish have a strong work ethic, and their natural austerity keeps overheads low. The church hopes to convince wealthy members to use money for unity within the community, and tolerates business as long as it remains small and local.

Until recently, accepted uses of money were limited to horse and other stock purchases, community mutual aid, and health care. As the Amish receive no social security, pensions, or health cover, and carry no commercial insurance policies,

The whole community is involved in a barn-raising.

they need money for doctors, dentists, and veterinary surgeons. Traditionally, they rely on spontaneous mutual aid and almsgiving within their community.

Probably the best-known form of Amish mutual aid is barn-raising. A team of about sixty men clear the site, and an Amish expert on barn building designs the new barn and orders the materials. A small crew builds the skeleton, then a large group returns for the actual raising. The barn owner pays for materials, but labor is given voluntarily. Amish women cook and serve food during the raising. Like other communal Amish projects, a barn-raising is to be enjoyed and is even called a "frolic." Mutual aid is concerned not just with economic security but with community spirit.

> ## Economic realities mean the Amish must find ways to compromise with the outside world.

Making the Quilt

THE LANCASTER ROSE IS FREQUENTLY constructed using two different fabrics for the outer edge of the petal and the central area. Here, crosshatched quilting fills the petal's center to create the same effect, making the pattern simpler for those who are not experienced at appliqué. To make a larger quilt, simply create more rose blocks.

CUTTING GUIDE

Piece	Quantity	Measurement
Background	1 cream	24 in (61 cm) square
Leaf shape A	4 green	see template page 121
Petal shape B	4 red	see template page 121
Circle shape C	2 yellow	see template page 121
Heart shape D	4 red	see template page 121
Border strips	4 green	3³/₈ x 26 in (8.5 x 66 cm)

See page 126 for the total amount of fabric required to complete this quilt.

CUTTING AND MARKING

1 Make full-size templates for the different components of the flower. Draw the full pattern *(see page 121)* on tracing paper and transfer it onto the background square. Draw inside the double lines of the pattern to mark a rough position guide on the backing fabric.

2 Transfer the template for shape A to card or plastic. Cut four leaves from green fabric including the seam allowances, and four smaller ones from support papers (along the seam allowance).

3 Transfer the two templates for the central ring onto card or template plastic. Cut out both circles and mark the inner cutting line and the stitching line *(see inset)*. Do not cut out the center yet.

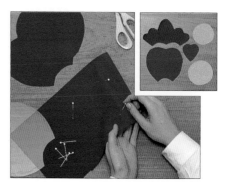

4 Trace the template for shape B onto card or plastic and draw round it on red fabric. Pin layers of fabric together and cut out four petals. *Inset:* Cut out shape D. All the elements are now ready.

STITCHING

5 Pin and baste (tack) the outer edges of each fabric leaf to a paper leaf, leaving the bottom edge open. Snip into the seam allowance where necessary to ease the fabric into place.

6 Pin a basted leaf in position on the background fabric following the marked lines.

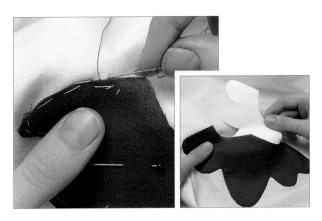

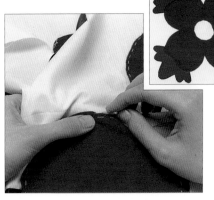

7 With matching thread, secure the leaf edges using small slipstitches, leave the base of the leaf open. *Inset:* Remove the pins and basting and carefully slide the backing paper out. Repeat for all the leaves.

8 Pin a petal in place, covering the raw bottom edge of its leaf. Baste 1/4 inch (6 mm) from the outside edges, leaving the bottom edge of the petal open. With the point of the needle, turn under the raw edge up to the basting and slipstitch with matching thread. Apply the second petal opposite the first and repeat, then add the final two petals to complete the flower *(see inset)*.

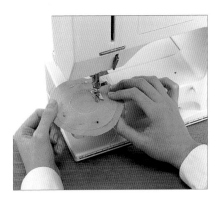

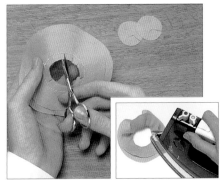

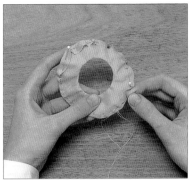

9 Stitch the two yellow circles together along the marked stitching line in the center, with right sides together.

10 Cut out the center with a small pair of scissors following the marked line. Clip the seam allowance. *Inset:* Turn the ring right sides out and press.

11 Turn under the raw edge of the top ring and pin and baste the fabric in place.

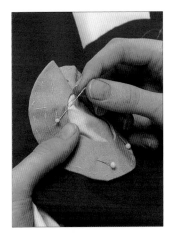

12 Pin the center ring in place. With matching thread, slipstitch first the inner then the outer seams, covering the raw edges of the petals as you work. Remove the basting and press.

13 Apply the border strips to the edges of the background square. Stitch the two opposite sides first, then add the remaining sides, making a 1/4-inch (6-mm) seam.

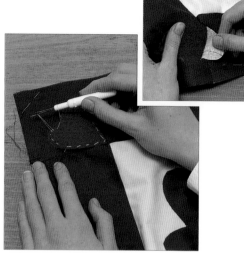

14 Next, add the appliqué hearts. Baste the paper template to the fabric for the heart and pin in position.

15 Slipstitch the heart in place, leaving a gap along one edge. Remove the basting threads. *Inset*: Carefully remove the paper and finish stitching.

16 Press the top from the wrong side. The Lancaster Rose is now ready to be marked with the quilting patterns.

MARKING

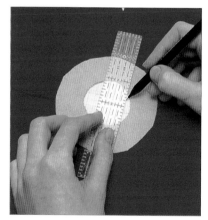

17 Mark crosshatching ¼ inch (6 mm) apart in the middle of the center ring using a pencil. Mark the inner line on the petal using the motif on page 125, then mark crosshatching at ½-inch (1.3-cm) intervals across the petal. Outline quilt the hearts and leaves in cream ¼ inch (6 mm) from the seam.

18 Using the motifs on page 123 and 125, mark the hearts and the diamond shapes following the diagram above. Bind the quilt using the bagging method on page 116. Slipstitch the opening and work the quilting.

Templates and Cutting

*T*HERE ARE TWO OCCASIONS ON which you may need to make templates. The first is for cutting multiple copies of patchwork or appliqué pieces that do not conform to geometric shapes; the second is for marking quilting patterns or motifs on the quilt top. First trace or create the required shape on paper, then re-draft it on thin cardboard or template plastic. There is a wide selection of markers available, from chalk and lead pencils to temporary water-soluble pens and colored pencils.

MAKING TEMPLATES

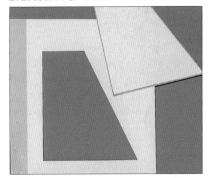

1 To make a window template that includes the cutting line and the seam allowance in one piece, draw the finished shape, excluding the seam allowance, on cardboard and cut it out carefully with a craft knife.

2 Place the shape on template plastic and draw around it. Then add a ¹/4-inch (6-mm) seam allowance around all edges. We have used a quilter's quarter to ensure accuracy.

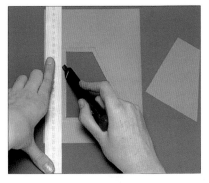

3 Using a craft knife and metal ruler, cut out the inner window and then the extended template around the outer edge. The inner window can be used to mark seams on fabric and to make support papers where these are used.

QUILTING TEMPLATES

1 Printed quilting patterns can be enlarged or reduced to fit a particular project and then traced onto template plastic or thin cardboard and cut out carefully.

2 Lay the template on the fabric and draw around it. A quilter's marking pencil is ideal for marking light-colored fabrics.

3 Chalk is one option for marking dark fabrics, but remember that it tends to rub off quickly, so erasing your pattern. Soapstone or silver marking pencils are also appropriate.

CUTTING OUT BY HAND

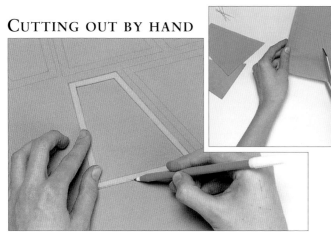

1 To use a window template, align the edges of the template with the fabric grain. Remember that the outer line is the cutting line; the inner line is the stitching line. Draw around only the outer line if you are stitching by machine; draw in the inner line if you are hand piecing. *Inset*: Cut out each fabric piece along the outer line. If you are using support papers, cut the papers along the inner line and pin a paper to each fabric piece.

CUTTING MULTIPLES

1 Some pieces are easier to cut using a paper pattern like a dressmaker's pattern. Pin the pattern to the fabric. It is not necessary to cut the paper pattern out before cutting the fabric pieces.

2 It is possible to cut two or more layers at once, but make sure you always use sharp dressmaker's scissors. The excess paper will simply fall away with the cut-off fabric.

ROTARY CUTTING

1 Fold the washed and pressed fabric along the straight grain so it fits on the cutting mat and level off the edge to be cut. Always place the ruler over the "good" fabric to avoid cutting into it, and cut away from your body.

2 Turn the trimmed fabric so the ruler covers the area you want to end up with. Use the markings on either the ruler or the mat – never both – to measure, then cut strips along the grain and usually across the width.

3 To cut stitched strips, first press the seams to one side and lay the finished strip right side up on the mat. Align the ruler with one or more seams and cut pieced strips of the desired width.

Hand and Machine Piecing

*P*ATCHWORK CAN BE JOINED BY hand or by machine. Many patterns are simple to stitch in strips on a machine, and many Amish quilters, who eschew most modern machines, use hand- or treadle-powered versions. However, the pleasure and accuracy of hand sewing still has great appeal for many people, and there are a number of patterns, such as those with curved or bias seams, that are easier to work by hand, but the seamlines must be marked on the wrong side of each piece.

HAND STITCHING – STRAIGHT SEAMS

1 Straight seams may be on the straight grain or on the bias. Mark the seam allowances carefully on each piece and pin two pieces right sides together.

2 Use a running stitch or backstitch to stitch along the marked seamline, taking care not to stretch the fabric as you work.

HAND STITCHING – FOUR-PIECE SEAMS

1 Sewing over seams by hand can be tricky. Here, two squares are stitched along the marked seamline and another pair is joined the same way.

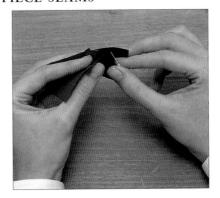

2 Fingerpress *(see page 115)* the joined units and pin the two pairs right sides together, making sure the seam allowances face in opposite directions.

3 Sew from the center seam out to one side and then to the other. *Inset:* The seams meet squarely in the middle, both on the front and on the back.

MACHINE STITCHING – STRIPS

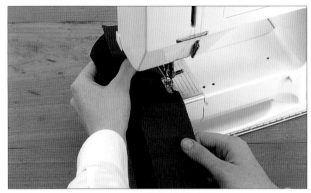

To join strips, place two right sides together, lining up the edges to be sewn, and make a straight 1/4-inch (6-mm) seam down the entire length of the strips. These strips can be cut into pieced units and combined in a variety of ways.

JOINING PIECED UNITS

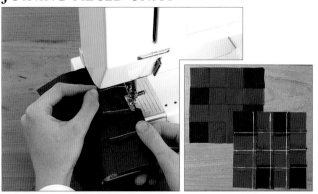

To combine pieced units, align the edges to be joined, right sides together. *Inset:* The joined unit has evenly matched rows with squared-up corners at each meeting point, front and back.

CHAIN-PIECING

1 To make a series of identical units, you can chain-piece by feeding the pieces through the machine one after the other without lifting the foot or breaking the thread.

2 The resulting chain of units, held together by short threads, can now be cut apart. This method can be used to speed up the piecing process.

FINGERPRESSING SEAMS

Short seams used to join patchwork pieces can be simply pressed with a finger or thumb, especially in the early stages. Try to make the seams lie flat, but do not pull so hard that you stretch the fabric.

Finishing Techniques

QUILTS TRADITIONALLY CONSIST of three layers: the top, which is usually pieced together as patchwork; the middle, which is a padded layer of batting (wadding); and the backing, which is usually a plain fabric. There are a number of ways of finishing a quilt, depending on how you are quilting and binding it. Most Amish quilts are singly bound after they have been quilted. Bagging is a way of backing and finishing the edges in the same operation, before quilting.

BACKING AND BATTING

Backing fabric should match or coordinate with the quilt top and must be of a weight and weave that makes it easy to quilt, particularly if you are hand-quilting. Batting, wadding, is the padded material used in the middle of a quilt to provide warmth and softness. It is available in various weights and materials off the roll like fabric or in ready-cut packs.

The backing and batting should both be larger than the top as the quilting draws them up. For a large quilt, to avoid having a

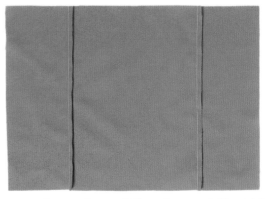

seam down the middle, place a full width of fabric in the center and add a narrower panel on each side as shown.

BAGGING

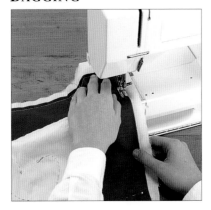

1 Place the top right side up on the batting, then place the backing fabric right side down on the top. Pin the edges all around and stitch a ¹/₄-inch (6-mm) seam. Leave a gap in the center of one side large enough to turn the quilt right side out.

2 Trim away the excess backing and batting. Always allow extra batting and backing all around the quilt.

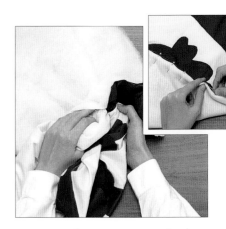

3 Trim the corners and turn the quilt right side out through the gap. Push the corners out from inside the quilt to make sure they are square. *Inset:* Pin and slipstitch the gap to close it. The quilt is now ready to be quilted.

BASTING

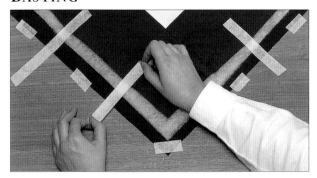

1 To bind the edges after you have worked the quilting, you must baste (tack) or pin the layers together first. Lay the backing wrong side up, cover it with the batting, and place the top right side up on the layers. Tape the edges to the working surface all around.

2 Use a long needle and long lengths of thread to baste the layers together, working from the center out and smoothing the layers as you work. Placing a spoon where the needle will come out makes it easier to sew through all the layers. The quilt is ready to be quilted.

BINDING

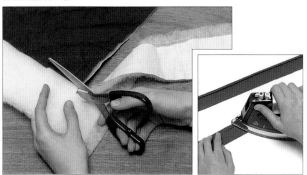

1 When all the quilting has been worked, trim the batting and backing level with the edges of the top. *Inset:* Cut strips twice the desired width plus 1/2-inch (1.3-cm) seam allowance along the straight grain. Press a 1/4-inch (6-mm) seamline along one edge of each strip.

2 Turn under 1/2 inch (1.3 cm) at one end of the binding strip and pin it along the edge of the quilt on the unpressed edge of the binding strip. Repeat to apply a strip to the opposite edge of the quilt.

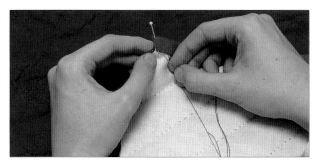

3 Turn the binding strip to the back of the quilt and pin in place with the pressed edge turned under. Slipstitch the binding in place; repeat on the opposite side of the quilt.

4 Apply a strip along the two unbound edges of the quilt in the same way, making sure you cover the end of the bound corners so there are no raw edges.

Patchwork Templates

The templates in this section are shown full-size. Some templates are shown as
halves. To make a full-size pattern for these pieces, place the dotted line on the fold of a piece
of tracing paper and trace the first half. Then turn the paper over and trace the other side
of the fold to make the second half. Open the paper and cut out the pattern.

DOUBLE WEDDING RING (page 70)

Be sure to transfer the dots precisely for
matching seams. The arc can be traced
and used as a guide to check the piecing
of Shapes A and B.

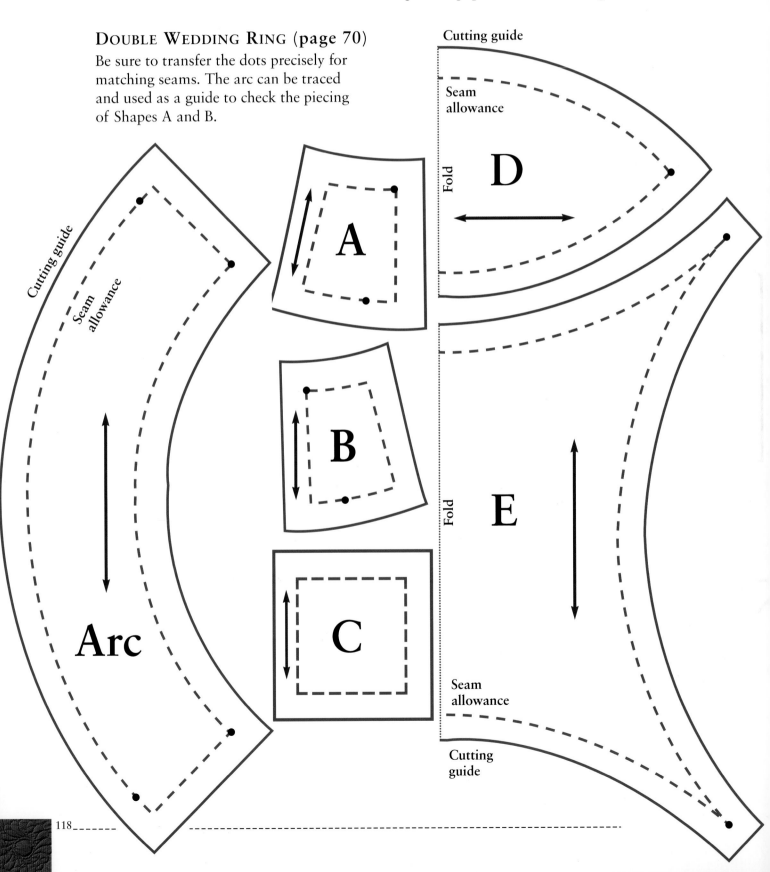

Cutting guide

Seam allowance

Fold

D

Cutting guide

Seam allowance

A

Cutting guide

Seam allowance

Arc

B

Fold

E

C

Seam allowance

Cutting guide

SCHOOLHOUSE
(page 80)

Place the fold of piece C on the straight grain. If using patterned fabric, flip template I to ensure that the pattern is right-side up.

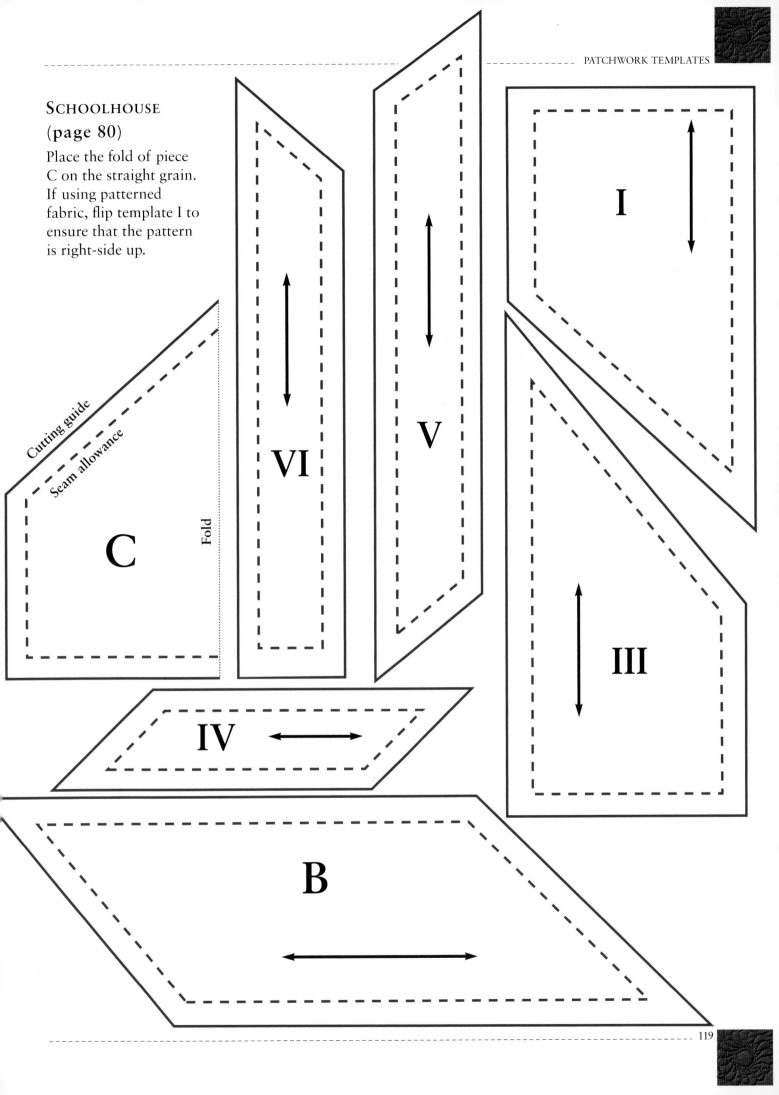

Cutting guide

Seam allowance

C

Fold

VI

V

I

IV

III

B

STARFLOWER (page 98)

Follow the arrows for the straight grain carefully to minimize stretching.

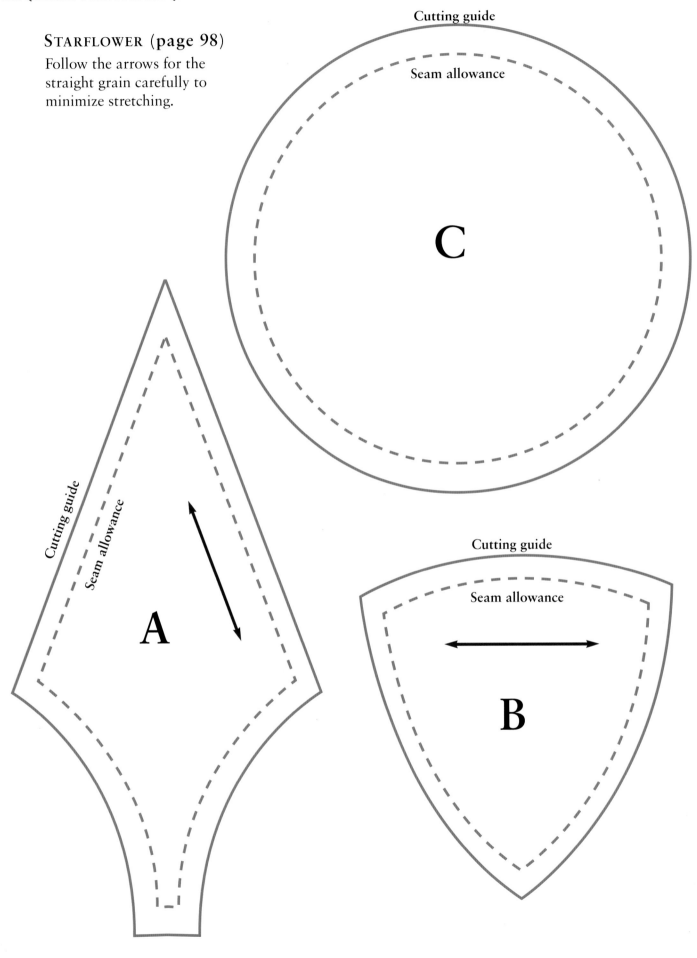

Cutting guide

Seam allowance

C

Cutting guide

Seam allowance

A

Cutting guide

Seam allowance

B

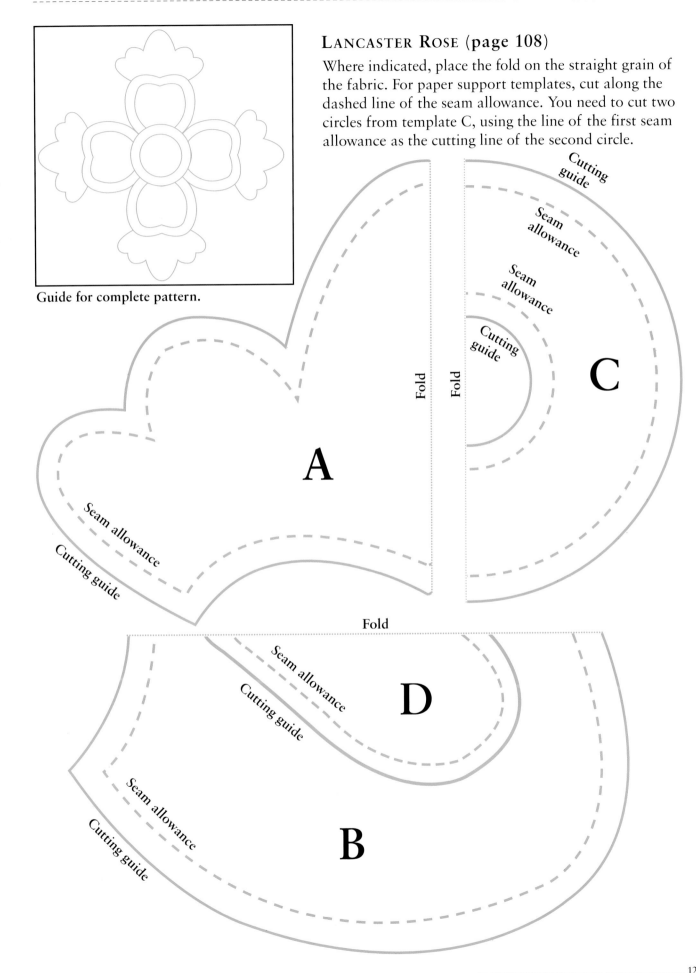

Guide for complete pattern.

LANCASTER ROSE (page 108)

Where indicated, place the fold on the straight grain of the fabric. For paper support templates, cut along the dashed line of the seam allowance. You need to cut two circles from template C, using the line of the first seam allowance as the cutting line of the second circle.

Quilting Motifs

To use the motifs the same size as those used in
the projects, enlarge them on a photocopier
by 120 percent, unless otherwise stated.

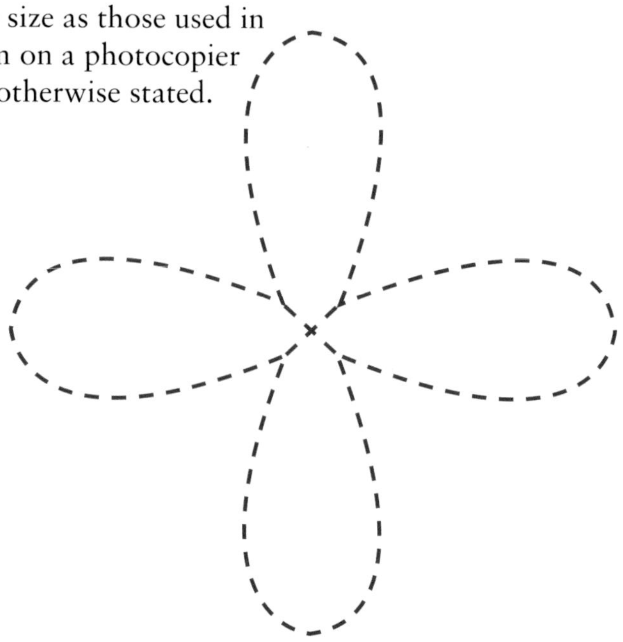

Double Wedding Ring – Flower
*Stitch this simple four-petaled
flower as two figure-eights,
starting in the center.*

Bars – Corner flower
*The outlines of this
motif can be traced
and the inner curves
of the petals drawn
freehand.*

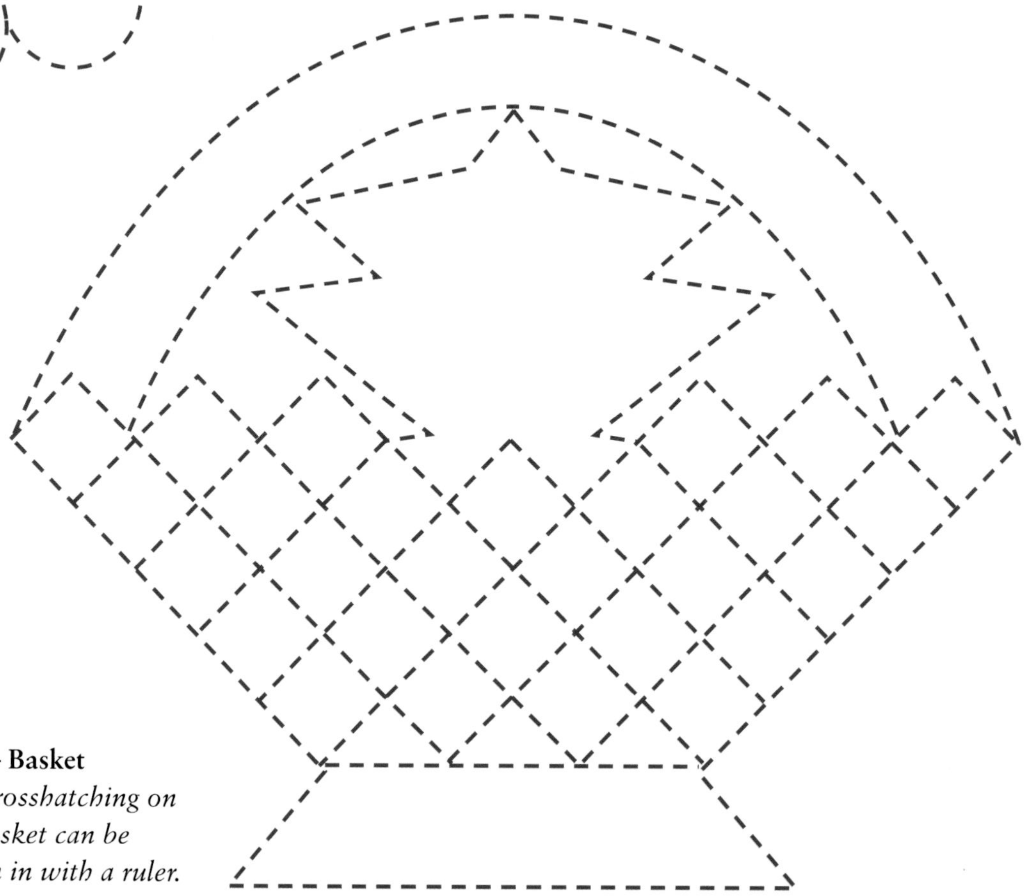

Bars – Basket
*The crosshatching on
the basket can be
drawn in with a ruler.*

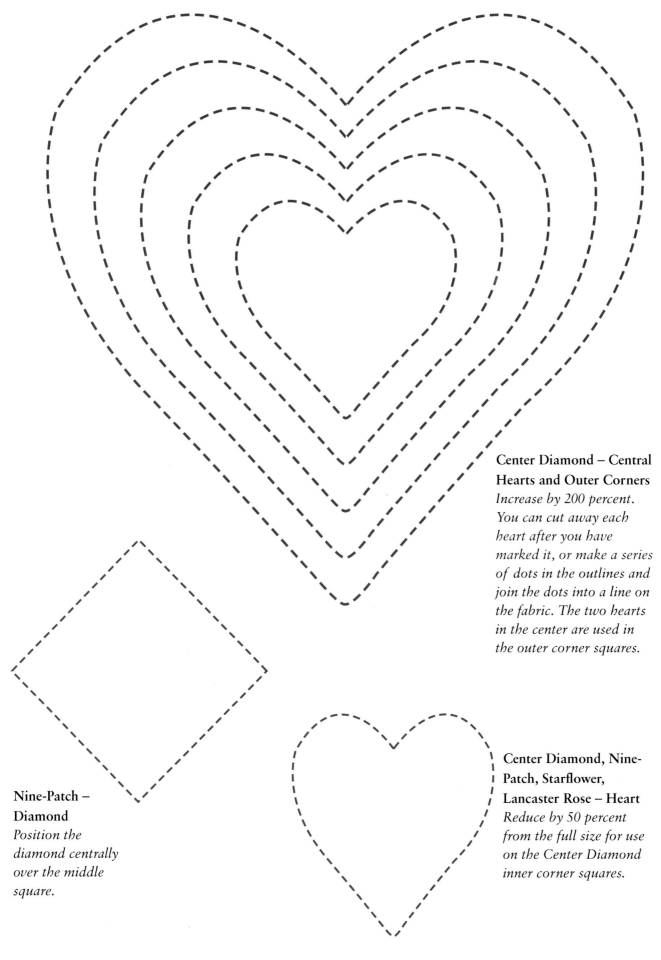

Center Diamond – Central Hearts and Outer Corners
Increase by 200 percent. You can cut away each heart after you have marked it, or make a series of dots in the outlines and join the dots into a line on the fabric. The two hearts in the center are used in the outer corner squares.

Nine-Patch – Diamond
Position the diamond centrally over the middle square.

Center Diamond, Nine-Patch, Starflower, Lancaster Rose – Heart
Reduce by 50 percent from the full size for use on the Center Diamond inner corner squares.

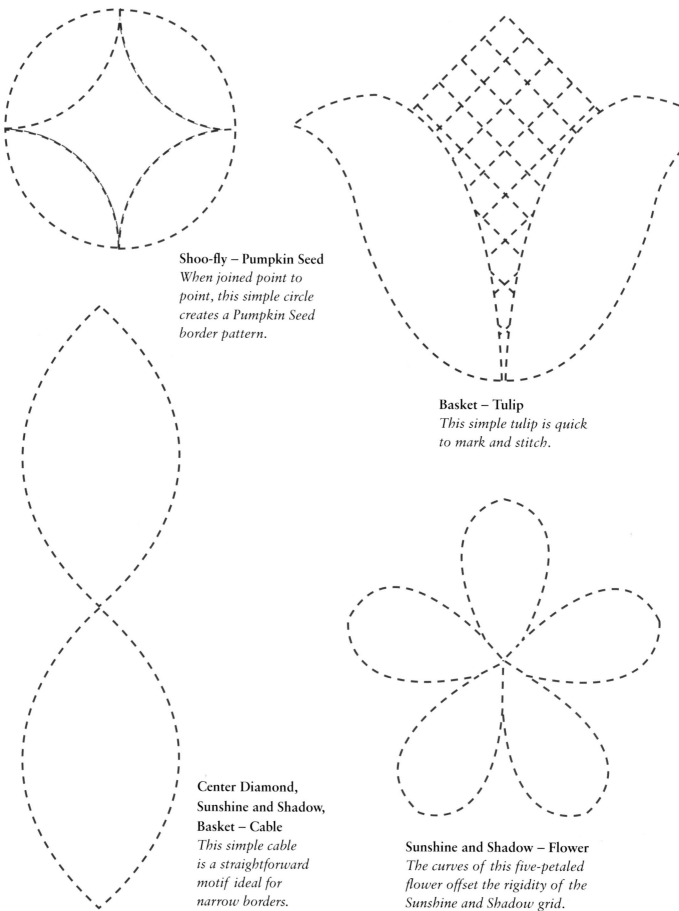

Shoo-fly – Pumpkin Seed
When joined point to point, this simple circle creates a Pumpkin Seed border pattern.

Basket – Tulip
This simple tulip is quick to mark and stitch.

Center Diamond, Sunshine and Shadow, Basket – Cable
This simple cable is a straightforward motif ideal for narrow borders.

Sunshine and Shadow – Flower
The curves of this five-petaled flower offset the rigidity of the Sunshine and Shadow grid.

Starflower – Border Pattern
Use the slanted line to match the corners.

Sunshine and Shadow – Double Cable
Repeat this pattern all along the outer border.

**Lancaster Rose –
Diamond**
*Link the outer points of
the diamond shapes to
create the outer border.*

Lancaster Rose – Petal
*Stitch along the curved
outer edges of the
petal. The bottom line
is not quilted.*

Fabric Quantities

All measurements are based on 44-inch (112-cm) wide fabric.
NB: Many designs can be sewn using scraps instead of the strip-piecing methods shown in the projects.

PROJECT	FINISHED SIZE	ELEMENTS	BACKING AND BATTING
BARS	42 in (107 cm) square	Red $1/2$ yd (50 cm) Blue 1 yd (90 cm) Purple $1/2$ yd (50 cm) Green $1/4$ yd (25 cm)	Blue 44 in (112 cm) square
CENTER DIAMOND	36 in (91 cm) square	Blue 15 in (38 cm) square Black $1/2$ yd (50 cm) square Green $1/4$ yd (25 cm) Pink scraps – 4 x 2 in (5 cm) squares Burgundy $7/8$ yd (90 cm)	Black 39 in (1 m) square
SUNSHINE AND SHADOW	51 in (130 cm) square	Colors 1–12 – $1/4$ yd (25 cm) each Color 13 – scraps 4 x 2 in (5 cm) square Color 14 – scraps 1 x 2 in (5 cm) square Purple $1/2$ yd (50 cm) Green $3/4$ yd (75 cm)	Calico 55 in (140 cm) square
NINE-PATCH	$13 1/2$ x 35 in (34 x 89 cm)	Dark blue $1/8$ yd (15 cm) Green – $1/8$ yd (15 cm) or $1 1/2$ x 18 in (4 x 46 cm) Purple – $1/8$ yd (15 cm)or $1 1/2$ x 18 in (4 x 46 cm) Red – $1/8$ yd (15 cm) or $1 1/2$ x 18 in (4 x 46 cm) Light Blue – $1/8$ yd (15 cm) or $1 1/2$ x 18 in (4 x 46 cm) Turquoise – $1/8$ yd (15 cm) or $1 1/2$ x 18 in (4 x 46 cm) Black $3/8$ yd (35 cm)	Dark blue 15 x 36 in (38 x 91 cm)
SHOO-FLY	40 x 55 in (102 x 140 cm)	6 contrasting colors – scraps 3 x 5 in (13 cm) squares Turquoise $7/8$ yd (80 cm) Navy $5/8$ yd (55 cm) Salmon – scraps 4 x $3 1/2$ in (9 cm) squares Purple – scraps 4 x $4 1/2$ in (11.5 cm) squares	Navy 44 x 60 in (112 x 152 cm)
DOUBLE WEDDING RING	21 in (53 cm) square at the widest points	Yellow – scraps maximum 24 x $1 1/2$ in (4 cm) squares Gold – scraps Light green – scraps Dark green – scraps Red – scraps Calico $1/4$ yd (25 cm)	Calico 23 in (58 cm) square
SCHOOLHOUSE	42 x 43 in (107 x 109 cm)	Red 1 yd (90 cm) Cream $5/8$ yd (60 cm)	Red 44 x 45 in (112 x 114 cm)
BASKET	$28 1/2$ in (72 cm) square	Rust $1/2$ yd (50 cm) 4 contrasting colors – scraps 1 x $4 3/4$ in (12 cm) square Black $1/2$ yd (50 cm)	Black 32 in (81 cm) square
STARFLOWER	28 in (71 cm) square	Red $1/4$ yd (25 cm) Blue $3/4$ yd (70 cm) Green $1/2$ yd (50 cm) Purple $1/4$ yd (25 cm)	Blue 30 in (76 cm) square
LANCASTER ROSE	26 in (66 cm) square	Cream 24 in (61 cm) square Green $3/4$ yd (70 cm) Red $3/8$ yd (30 cm) Yellow – scraps 2 x 4 in (10 cm) squares	Cream 30 in (76 cm) square

Index

Acknowledgments

Authors' Acknowledgments

We would like to thank everyone involved in this very personal project, especially Sarah Hoggett for her enthusiasm, Katie Bent and Julia Ward-Hastelow for their encouragement, Matthew Ward for the superb photographs, Kate Simunek for the beautiful illustrations, and Tiffany Jenkins for her helping hands. Thanks also to Brenda Ross for her encouragement, and to Rebecca Arscott who quilted the Sunshine and Shadow and Center Diamond projects, and Joan Everard who quilted the Shoo-fly quilt.

Many thanks to Ruth and Jim Finley, Jan's parents, for their help with quilts and contacts, and our abiding thanks to the Amish women of Lancaster County for their wonderful needlework.

Publisher's Acknowledgments

The Publisher would like to thank Lisa Dyer, Geraldine Christy, and Hilary Bird for their helpful suggestions and contributions. Also, many thanks to Alison Lee and Claire Graham.

Thanks to the Bogod Machine Company, London,
for supplying the sewing machine used in the projects.